LEARN TO DRAW

Celebrated Characters COLLECTION

Including your Disney · PIXAR **Favorites!**

7 9 10 8

Tools and Materials

Before you begin your drawing, you will need to gather a few simple tools. Start with a regular pencil so you can easily erase any mistakes. Make sure to have an eraser and pencil sharpener too! When you're finished with your drawing, you can bring your characters to life by adding color—just grab some colored pencils, markers, or even watercolor or acrylic paints.

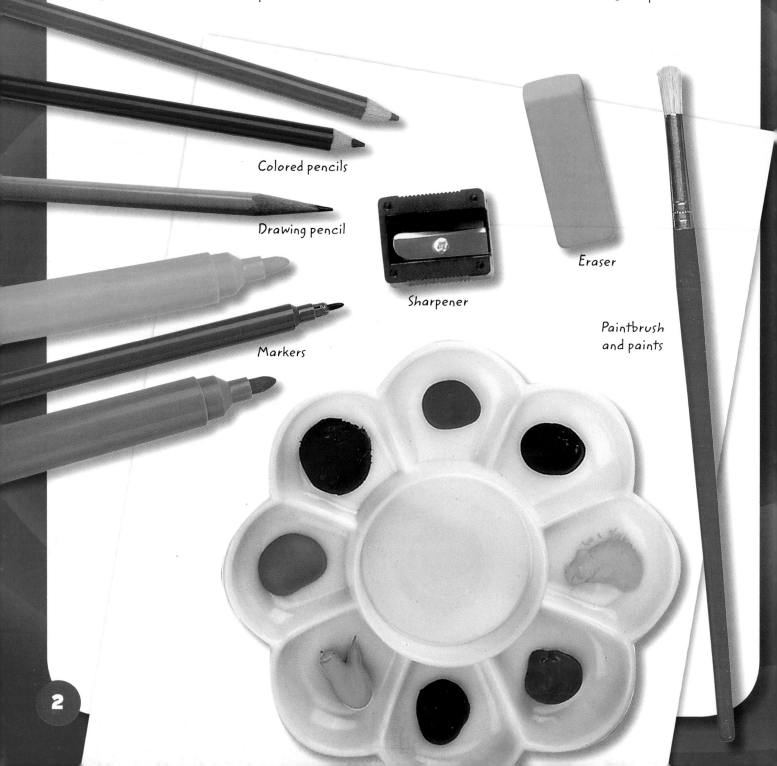

Colored pencils

Drawing pencil

Markers

Sharpener

Eraser

Paintbrush and paints

Warm-Up Exercises

Before you get started, warm up your hand by drawing some squiggles and shapes on a piece of scrap paper.

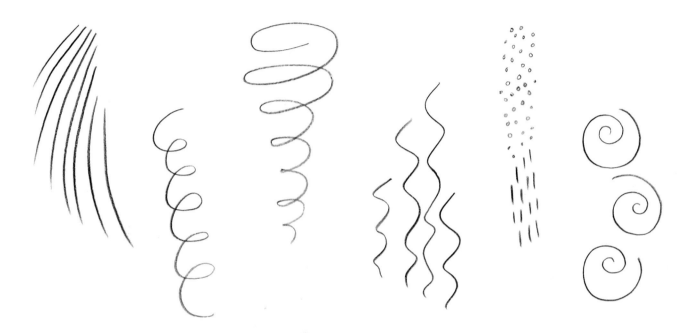

Practice drawing circles.

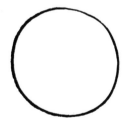

Practice drawing squares.

Practice drawing triangles.

Practice drawing rectangles.

Practice drawing ovals.

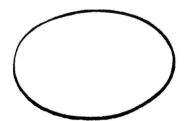

Getting Started

Usually artists draw characters in several steps. Sometimes the steps are different, depending on what you're drawing. The important thing to remember is to start simply and add details later. The blue lines show each new step, and the black lines show what you've already drawn.

1

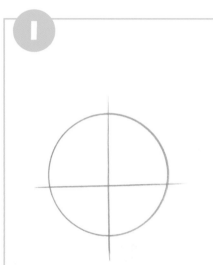

The first thing you'll draw are guidelines to help position the features of the character.

2

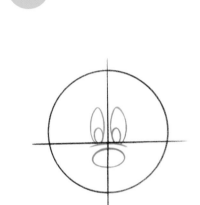

Next you'll start to add details to your drawing. It will take several steps to add all the details.

3

When you finish all the details of your drawing, you can go back and erase your guidelines. You can also darken your lines with a pen or marker.

Donald has learned all the steps, and now he's ready to color the finished drawing!

LEARN TO DRAW

MICKEY MOUSE

Illustrated and Designed by
John Loter and the
Disney Publishing
Creative Development Staff

MICKEY MOUSE

Drawing Mickey's Face

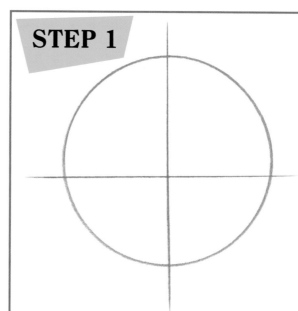

Start with a circle. Add center lines to help position Mickey's features.

STEP 2

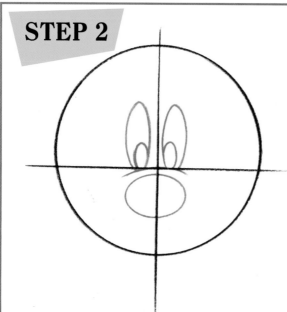

Now add Mickey's eyes and nose. His eyes rest on the edge of one center line. Add a little curve right below his eyes.

STEP 3

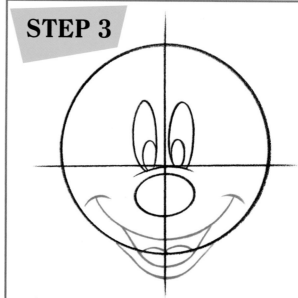

Add Mickey's smile and chin. The top portion of his mouth follows the same curve as his nose. See how his chin extends below the circle of his head.

Pluto is Mickey's favorite pup, and Mickey is Pluto's best pal.

STEP 4

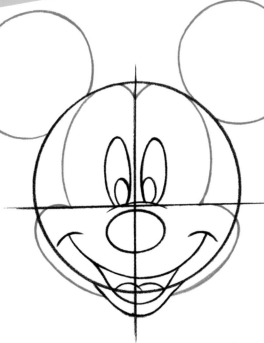

Draw two large ovals for Mickey's ears. Add curved lines to form the area around his cheeks and eyes. (This is called the "mask.")

STEP 5

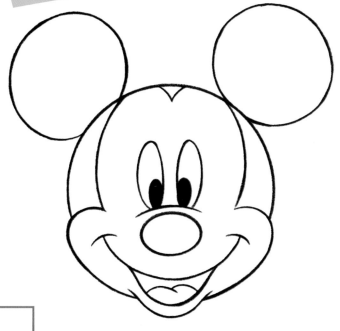

Erase your guidelines and clean up the drawing.

STEP 6

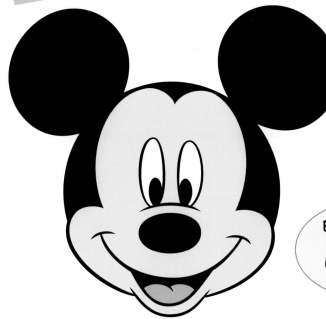

Now color your drawing of Mickey.

BE SURE TO MAKE HIM HANDSOME!

MICKEY MOUSE
Drawing Mickey's Head

Start with a circle. Add center lines to help position Mickey's features.

STEP 2

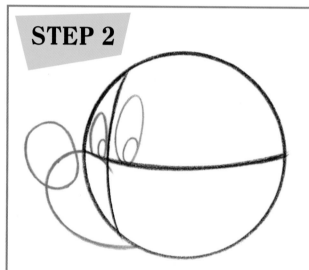

Add Mickey's eyes and nose. His eyes rest on the edge of one center line. For his nose, draw a curved line for the snout. Position the bulb of his nose on the end.

STEP 3

Add Mickey's smile and chin. The top of his smile follows the curve of his nose. See how his chin extends below the circle of his head.

Mickey's eyebrows can show how he's feeling.

STEP 4

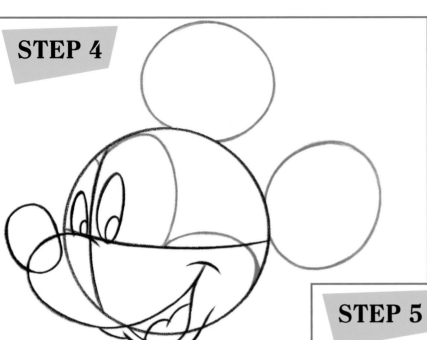

Draw two large ovals for Mickey's ears. In this view, one of Mickey's ears is on the top of his head, and the other is on the back. Add curved lines to form the mask.

You can always see both of Mickey's ears, no matter which direction his head is turned.

STEP 5

Erase your guidelines and clean up the drawing.

STEP 6

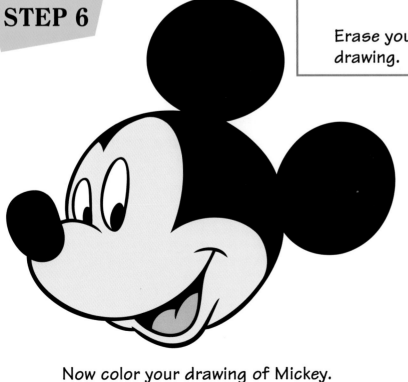

Now color your drawing of Mickey.

When Mickey is surprised, his ears go up.

MINNIE MOUSE
Drawing Minnie's Face

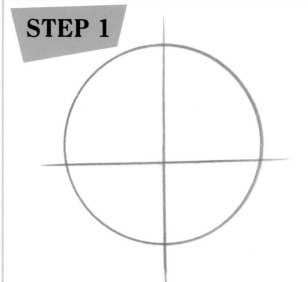

Start with a circle. Add center lines to help position Minnie's features, just as you did for Mickey.

STEP 2

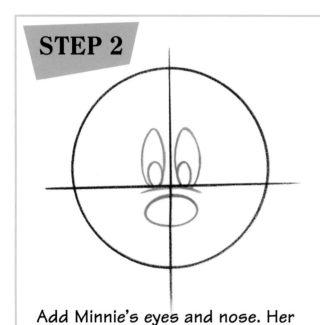

Add Minnie's eyes and nose. Her eyes rest on the edge of one center line.

STEP 3

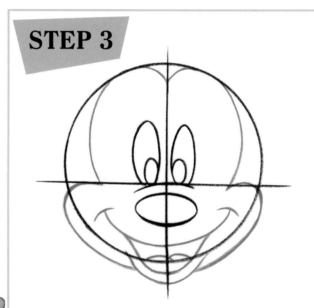

Add Minnie's smile and chin. The top portion of her mouth follows the same curve as her nose. See how her chin extends below the circle of her head. Add curved lines to form the mask.

Minnie and Daisy are the very best of friends.

STEP 4

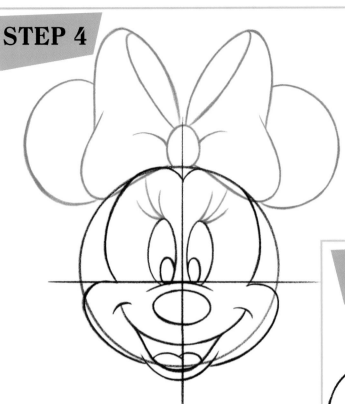

Draw two large ovals for Minnie's ears and a great big bow on top of her head. Don't forget her eyelashes!

Don't forget Minnie's eyelashes. The middle lashes are longer than the others.

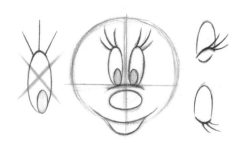

STEP 5

Erase your guidelines and clean up the drawing.

STEP 6

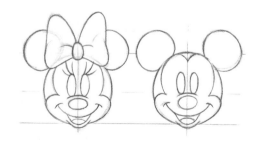

Minnie's and Mickey's heads are similar, but Minnie's eyes are slightly larger and wider than Mickey's. Her open mouth is slightly smaller than his.

DONALD DUCK

Drawing Donald's Face

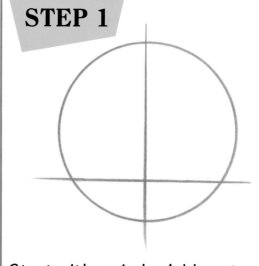

Start with a circle. Add center lines to help position the features.

STEP 2

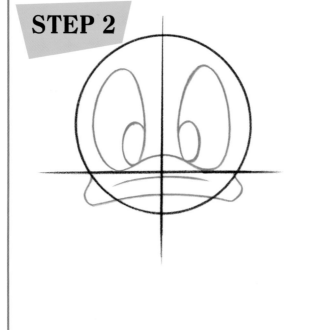

STEP 3

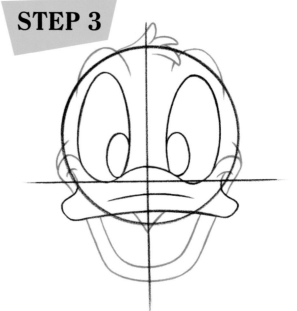

Add Donald's eyebrows and tufts on the top of his head. See how his lower bill curves below his head. His cheeks are very curvy when he smiles. Now add a little triangle for his tongue.

Goofy's silly attitude sometimes irritates the hot-tempered Donald, but Mickey usually manages to keep the peace.

STEP 4

Add Donald's cap. See how the hatband and the ribbon are the same width.

STEP 5

Erase your guidelines and clean up the drawing.

Donald's hat is soft and flexible but always holds its shape.

STEP 6

Now color your drawing of Donald.

GAWRSH! THAT'S A FUNNY HAT!

DAISY DUCK

Drawing Daisy's Face

STEP 1

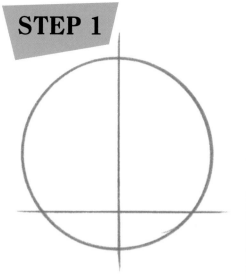

Start with a circle. Add cross lines to help position Daisy's features.

STEP 2

Add Daisy's eyes and the top of her bill. Notice how her eyes are rounder and more angled than Donald's. The bottoms of her eyes and the top of her bill fit together smoothly.

STEP 3

Add Daisy's eyebrows and the lower part of her bill. Now add the little triangle for her tongue, just as you did for Donald.

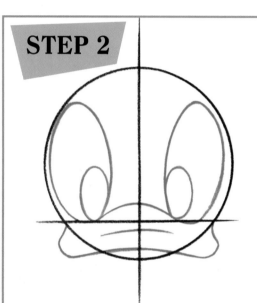

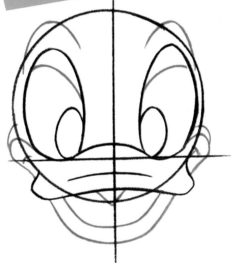

Daisy is just crazy for Donald.

STEP 4

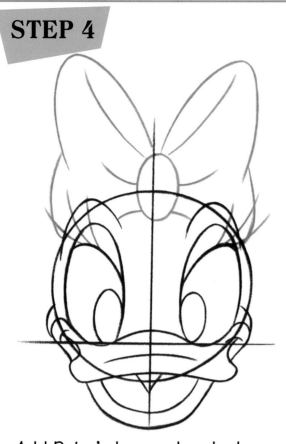

Add Daisy's bow and eyelashes. She has three eyelashes over each eye. The middle lashes are longer than the others.

STEP 5

Erase your guidelines and clean up the drawing.

STEP 6

Now color your drawing of Daisy.

BETTER SHARPEN YOUR PENCIL FOR DAISY'S EYELASHES!

GOOFY
Drawing Goofy's Face

Start with a circle. Then add cross lines as shown to help position Goofy's features. In this expression, part of Goofy's face is on an angle, so you'll make the center lines angled, too.

STEP 2

Add a squished oval beneath the circle for Goofy's nose. Then add his cheeks, teeth, and mouth.

STEP 3

Add Goofy's big oval eyes and tongue.

!?

Goofy's head is similar to Pluto's.

STEP 4

Add Goofy's hat and ears. His ears are like big teardrops.

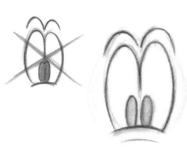

Notice how the whites of Goofy's eyes touch each other. Just make sure you keep his pupils separate.

STEP 5

Erase your guidelines and clean up the drawing.

STEP 6

Now color your drawing of Goofy.

Goofy's hat is about 1 head long. It's squishy looking and leans to one side.

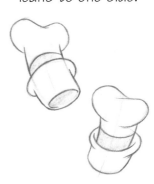

PLUTO
Drawing Pluto's Head

Start with a circle. Add center lines to help position Pluto's features. The circle for Pluto's head is much smaller than for the other characters.

STEP 2

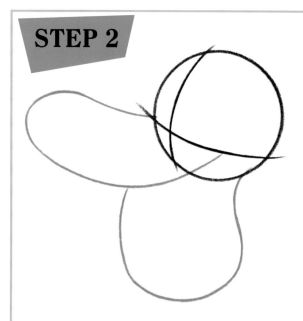

Sketch in the snout and lower jaw. Pluto has a long nose pointing forward and a long, rounded jaw dropping down from the circle of his head.

STEP 3

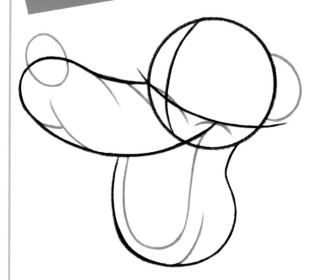

Add the details of Pluto's nose and mouth. Don't forget to add the knob on the back of his head.

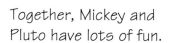

Together, Mickey and Pluto have lots of fun.

STEP 4

Add Pluto's eyes. eyebrows, and tongue. Pluto's eyes are long ovals, and his tongue hangs down from his mouth. Now add his ear.

STEP 5

Erase your guidelines and clean up the drawing.

STEP 6

Now color your drawing of Pluto.

ENOUGH, ALREADY! LET'S GO BACK TO PAGE 12!

How to Draw

Disney

Winnie the Pooh

Designed and Illustrated by the Disney Publishing
Creative Development Staff

21

Winnie the Pooh

Drawing Pooh's Face

Pooh is a bear of little brain and big tummy. He has a one-food mind when it comes to honey. But he is also a good friend to Piglet and a perfect pal for "doing nothing" with Christopher Robin. Pooh has a simple sweetness to him that goes beyond the honey stuck to his paws!

How do you draw Pooh's ears?

Too pointy!

Too round!

Pooh's nose is a soft triangle.

Just right!

Sometimes Disney artists look in the mirror to see how to draw certain expressions. If Pooh were drawing a picture of himself, he'd have a perfect model for a giggling bear!

Step 1

Draw a circle. Then draw two lines crossed in the middle of the circle.

Step 4

Now add his smile.

Step 2

Add Pooh's ears, eyes, and chin. Don't forget his eyebrows!

Step 3

Use the crossed lines to help you figure out where to draw Pooh's nose.

Step 5

Carefully erase the guidelines and clean up the drawing.

Step 6

Now color your picture!

Winnie the Pooh

Drawing Pooh's Body

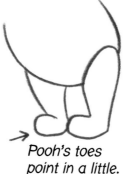

Pooh's toes point in a little.

Keep ears apart in profile.

Shirt is loose fittin'

Feet are soft and pliable to indicate toe area.

Step 1

Draw a circle for the head. Then add a pear shape below it for his body.

Step 2

Add Pooh's arms and legs.

Step 3

Use the blue lines to figure out where to put Pooh's eyes, nose, mouth, and shirt.

Piglet thinks the silly old bear is a wonderful friend.

Pooh is about 2-1/2 heads high.

Pooh can have a little thumb if he needs to grab something.

Pooh's arms are almost the same length as his legs.

Step 4

Add sleeves and a collar to Pooh's shirt.

Step 5

You can erase the extra lines when you finish your picture.

Step 6

Now color your drawing!

25

Tigger

Drawing Tigger's Face

Tigger surely is one of a kind in the Hundred-Acre Wood. He's a good bouncing buddy for little Roo, but his springy style bowls over the others. Tigger is always sure of "what tiggers do best," even before he does something. But perhaps the really "wonderful thing" about Tigger is the bounce he brings to everyone around him.

Use the crossed lines to help figure out where to draw Tigger's ears.

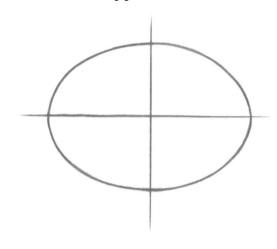

Tigger's ears are triangles about as wide as his nose.

When Tigger smiles, his eyes are single lines.

Being a very small animal, Piglet isn't always able to jump as high as his friend Tigger.

Step 4

Use curved lines to add Tigger's stripes and whiskers.

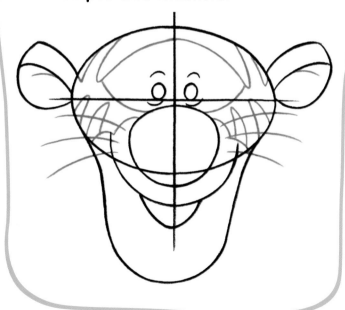

26

Step 2

Tigger's ears point up and out. Don't forget to draw Tigger's big chin.

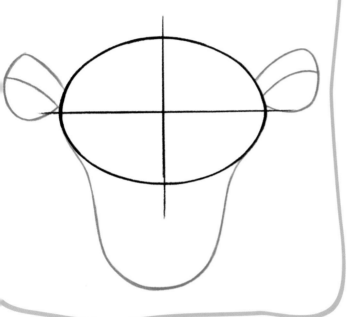

Step 3

Add Tigger's eyes and large nose. Then draw his big grin!

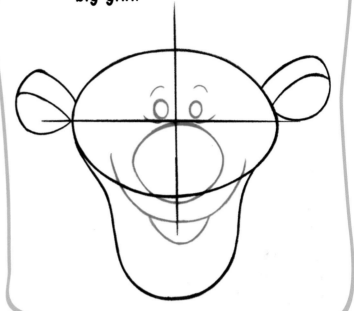

Step 5

Erase your guidelines and clean up the drawing.

Step 6

Color your picture of Tigger!

Tigger

Drawing Tigger's Body

Step 1

Tigger's body is a long oval with a short oval on top.

Step 2

Tigger's arms are much longer than his legs.

Step 3

The stripe pattern on Tigger's body varies. Use a mixture of large and small stripes.

His tail squishes when he bounces.

Step 4

Erase the construction lines and clean up the drawing.

Tigger's body is shaped like a banana.

Step 5

Color your picture!

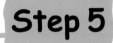

Poor Eeyore always seems to be losing his tail. He can't even imagine what it must be like to have a springy tail like Tigger's that never falls off, even with the bounciest of bounces.

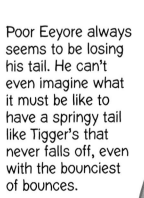

Piglet

Drawing Piglet's Head

Piglet is a very small animal. He is little enough to be swept away by a leaf and timid enough to be scared by Pooh's stories of "jagulars." His eyebrows and mouth usually show how he's feeling.

Piglet's head is peanut-shaped.

Make sure his ears don't point toward each other or he'll appear to have horns.

Being a small and timid animal, Piglet is often comforted by the strong and wise Christopher Robin.

Draw your circle, then the crossed lines.

Add floppy ears and a chubby cheek.

Step 2

Draw Piglet's long face with a point at the bottom.

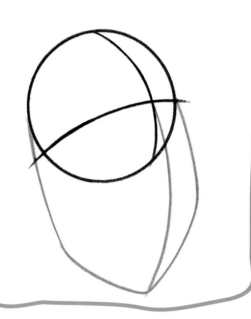

Step 3

Add Piglet's eyes, nose, and mouth along the crossed lines.

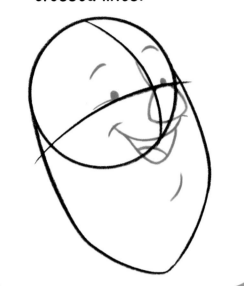

Step 5

Erase the construction lines and clean up the drawing.

Step 6

Now color the picture!

Eyore

Drawing Eyore's Head

Things are always looking down for Eyore. With a tail that comes loose and a house that falls down, he's always ready for things to go wrong. Still, Eyore manages to smile once in a while, even though he's almost always gloomy.

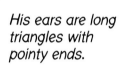

His ears are long triangles with pointy ends.

His mane falls forward.

Piglet, being a very small animal, is easily frightened.

Step 1

Draw a circle with crossed lines for the head.

Step 4

Little curved lines around Eyore's eyes make him look sad.

Step 2

Then add a shape like a sack for his nose.

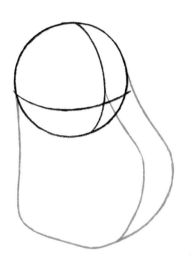

Step 3

Eeyore's ears, eyes, and eyebrows usually droop downward.

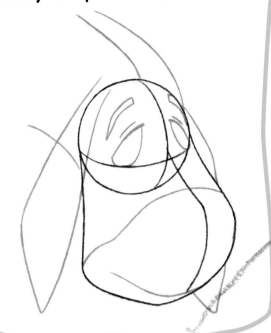

Step 5

Erase the construction lines and clean up the drawing.

Step 6

Color your picture of Eeyore!

Kanga & Roo

Drawing Kanga's & Roo's Bodies

Kanga is kind of like the mother to everyone in the Hundred-Acre Wood—but especially to her own little boy, Roo. Did you know that if you put Kanga's and Roo's names together they spell "KANGAROO"? And that is, of course, the kind of animal they are.

Kanga has a small, round head atop a body shaped like a kidney bean. Roo also has a round head—but it's even smaller.

Keep hands glovelike.

For Tigger, bouncing is fun, fun, fun! Roo agrees with his pal and tries to imitate Tigger's bouncing whenever he can.

Keep feet large and soft.

Step 2

Add Kanga's ears, arms, legs, and tail. Then draw the details of her face. Don't forget Roo's face too.

Step 3

Draw in the details of Kanga's and Roo's bodies.

Step 4

Carefully erase the construction lines and clean up the drawing.

Step 5

Now color the picture!

Disney · PIXAR

ILLUSTRATED BY THE DISNEY STORYBOOK ARTISTS
INSPIRED BY THE CHARACTER DESIGNS CREATED BY PIXAR ANIMATION STUDIOS

IT'S TIME FOR THE BIGGEST CAR RACE OF THE YEAR, THE DINOCO 400. IN THIS WORLD, CARS ARE THE CHARACTERS, AND ROOKIE SENSATION LIGHTNING MCQUEEN ROLLS OUT OF HIS TRAILER TO SWARMING REPORTERS AND CHEERING FANS.

THE WINNER OF THE RACE WILL GET THE COVETED PISTON CUP TROPHY. THE THREE TOP CONTENDERS ARE NINE-TIME PISTON CUP WINNER THE KING, PERENNIAL RUNNER-UP CHICK HICKS, AND NEW HOTSHOT LIGHTNING MCQUEEN. AND WITH THE KING RETIRING, HIS LUCRATIVE DINOCO SPONSORSHIP IS ALSO UP FOR GRABS.

LIGHTNING TAKES THE LEAD! BUT AT HIS PIT STOP, HE REFUSES TO CHANGE TIRES TO SAVE TIME. IT'S A BAD MOVE. IN THE FINAL LAP, HIS REAR TIRES BLOW! CHICK AND THE KING CATCH UP, AND THE RACE IS TOO CLOSE TO CALL!

WHILE THEY WAIT FOR THE RESULTS, THE KING TELLS LIGHTNING HE NEEDS TO TREAT HIS PIT CREW BETTER, BUT LIGHTNING ISN'T LISTENING. HE'S DAYDREAMING ABOUT HIS FUTURE GLORY . . . UNTIL HE LEARNS THE RACE WAS A THREE-WAY TIE! A TIE-BREAKER RACE WILL BE HELD IN CALIFORNIA IN ONE WEEK.

RELUCTANTLY LIGHTNING MAKES A QUICK APPEARANCE FOR RUST-EZE,

CAUSING LIGHTNING TO DRIVE WILDLY. HE TEARS UP THE ASPHALT STREET AND ENDS UP HANGING BETWEEN TWO TELEPHONE POLES.

THE NEXT MORNING, LIGHTNING WAKES UP IN THE TOWN IMPOUND. THE SHERIFF ORDERS THE FRIENDLY, RUSTY TOW TRUCK NAMED MATER TO TOW LIGHTNING TO TRAFFIC COURT.

IN COURT, SALLY, THE TOWN'S ATTORNEY, ARGUES THAT THE RUINED ROAD WILL TURN AWAY DESPERATELY NEEDED CUSTOMERS. DOC, THE JUDGE, SENTENCES LIGHTNING TO STAY UNTIL HE FIXES THE ROAD.

HIS CURRENT SPONSOR. THEN HE BACKS INTO HIS TRAILER AND HITS THE ROAD WITH HIS DRIVER, MACK. LIGHTNING PUSHES MACK TO DRIVE THROUGH THE NIGHT. HE WANTS TO BE THE FIRST TO REACH THE CALIFORNIA RACE. AFTER MANY LONG HOURS, MACK DOZES OFF. HE SWERVES AND LIGHTNING FALLS OUT OF THE TRAILER!

TERRIFIED, LIGHTNING DODGES THE ONCOMING TRAFFIC AND DESPERATELY FOLLOWS MACK DOWN AN OFF-RAMP—ONLY TO FIND IT ISN'T MACK HE WAS FOLLOWING! LOST AND PANICKED, LIGHTNING SPEEDS THROUGH THE SMALL TOWN OF RADIATOR SPRINGS. THE SHERIFF TAKES CHASE, MAKING BACKFIRE NOISES THAT SOUND LIKE GUNSHOTS,

LIGHTNING IS HOOKED TO THE MESSY PAVER NAMED BESSIE. AFTER AN HOUR HE SAYS HE'S FINISHED, BUT THE ROAD LOOKS TERRIBLE. DOC CHALLENGES LIGHTNING TO A RACE. IF LIGHTNING WINS, HE CAN GO. BUT IF LIGHTNING LOSES, HE WILL HAVE TO STAY AND FINISH THE ROAD DOC'S WAY.

WHEN THE RACE BEGINS, LIGHTNING LEAVES DOC IN THE DUST, SPEEDING AHEAD AND RIPPING AROUND A TURN . . . RIGHT OVER THE EDGE OF A DEEP DITCH AND INTO A CACTUS PATCH.

THAT NIGHT LIGHTNING GOES BACK TO WORK. BY MORNING, THERE IS A BEAUTIFUL, NEWLY PAVED STRETCH OF ROAD.

DOC FINDS LIGHTNING BACK AT THE DIRT TRACK TRYING TO GET THE TURN HE MISSED. HE TELLS LIGHTNING THAT IF HE RACES ON DIRT AND WANTS TO TURN LEFT, SOMETIMES HE SHOULD STEER RIGHT. LIGHTNING LAUGHS AT THE ADVICE, BUT WHEN NO ONE IS WATCHING HE TRIES IT . . . AND FALLS RIGHT INTO THE CACTUS PATCH AGAIN.

THE TOWNSFOLK ARE INSPIRED BY THE NEW STRETCH OF ROAD, SO THEY BEGIN FIXING UP THEIR SHOPS. THAT NIGHT, MATER TAKES LIGHTNING TRACTOR TIPPING. AND LIGHTNING IS HAVING FUN UNTIL A COMBINE CHASES THEM OFF!

BACK IN TOWN, SALLY OVERHEARS LIGHTNING EXPLAINING THAT WINNING THE PISTON CUP MEANS HE'LL HAVE FAME, FORTUNE, AND A BIG NEW SPONSOR. HE EVEN PROMISES MATER A HELICOPTER RIDE. THRILLED, MATER DECLARES LIGHTNING HIS BEST FRIEND.

LATER, SALLY APPROACHES LIGHTNING AND ASKS IF HE INTENDS TO KEEP HIS PROMISE TO MATER. FOLKS IN RADIATOR SPRINGS TRUST ONE ANOTHER, AND SHE DOESN'T WANT MATER TO GET HURT.

THE NEXT MORNING, MATER AWAKENS THE WHOLE TOWN TO SHOW THEM THAT THE ROAD IS FINISHED. THEN LIGHTNING GOES SHOPPING—AND HE BECOMES THE BEST CUSTOMER RADIATOR SPRINGS HAS SEEN IN A LONG TIME.

THE NEXT MORNING, LIGHTNING WANDERS INTO DOC'S BACK OFFICE, WHERE HE FINDS THREE PISTON CUPS AND REALIZES THAT DOC IS THE FABULOUS HUDSON HORNET! DOC IS FURIOUS THAT LIGHTNING HAS DISCOVERED HIS SECRET AND HE ANGRILY SHOOS AWAY LIGHTNING.

SALLY INVITES LIGHTNING ON A DRIVE UP THE MOUNTAIN. AT THE TOP, SALLY TELLS THE STORY OF HOW SHE LEFT LOS ANGELES AND FOUND HER HOME IN RADIATOR SPRINGS. SHE ALSO EXPLAINS HOW RADIATOR SPRINGS WAS BYPASSED WHEN THE INTERSTATE WAS BUILT. SHE'D GIVE ANYTHING TO HAVE SEEN IT IN ITS HEYDAY.

LATER, LIGHTNING SECRETLY WATCHES DOC GRACEFULLY RACING AT THE DIRT TRACK. WHEN DOC DISCOVERS LIGHTNING, HE LEAVES—BUT LIGHTNING FOLLOWS HIM. DOC FINALLY LETS OUT HIS SECRET: WHEN HE RETURNED TO THE RACING WORLD AFTER RECOVERING FROM A BIG WRECK, DOC WAS REPLACED BY A ROOKIE LIKE LIGHTNING.

THE NEXT MORNING, MATER AWAKENS THE WHOLE TOWN TO SHOW THEM THAT THE ROAD IS FINISHED. THEN LIGHTNING GOES SHOPPING—AND HE BECOMES THE BEST CUSTOMER RADIATOR SPRINGS HAS SEEN IN A LONG TIME.

SALLY IS TOUCHED THAT LIGHTNING HELPED ALL THE TOWNSFOLK. AS DUSK SETTLES, LIGHTNING CUES THE TOWNSFOLK TO TURN ON THEIR NEWLY REPAIRED NEON LIGHTS. RADIATOR SPRINGS IS JUST LIKE IT WAS IN ITS HEYDAY. EVERYONE CRUISES HAPPILY.

BUT THE MOOD IS CRUSHED BY AN INVASION OF REPORTERS. LIGHTNING HAS BEEN FOUND! MACK ARRIVES TO TAKE LIGHTNING TO THE BIG RACE. LIGHTNING FINDS SALLY IN THE CROWD. SPEECHLESS, HE LISTENS TO HER AS SHE WISHES HIM LUCK. THEN HE SADLY DRIVES INTO THE TRAILER AND LEAVES.

THE TIE-BREAKER RACE IS SET TO BEGIN. INSIDE HIS TRAILER, LIGHTNING TRIES TO PREPARE, BUT HIS HEART ISN'T IN IT. AS THE RACE BEGINS, LIGHTNING FALLS FAR BEHIND . . . UNTIL HE REALIZES ALL HIS PALS FROM RADIATOR SPRINGS HAVE COME TO BE HIS PIT CREW!

NEWLY DETERMINED, LIGHTNING CATCHES UP WITH THE LEADERS. HIS PIT CREW TAKES CARE OF HIM, FIXING A BLOWN TIRE. AND WHEN CHICK BUMPS INTO HIM, HE QUICKLY RECOVERS BY USING THE DIRT-TURN TRICK DOC TAUGHT HIM. SOON HE PULLS INTO FIRST PLACE!

WHEN CHICK CAUSES THE KING TO CRASH BEHIND HIM, LIGHTNING HEARS THE CROWD GASP AND LOOKS UP AT THE STADIUM SCREEN. THE IMAGE REMINDS HIM OF DOC'S CRASH. LIGHTNING SLAMS ON HIS BRAKES JUST BEFORE THE FINISH LINE.

CHICK WINS THE RACE BUT NO ONE CARES. LIGHTNING REVERSES AND PUSHES THE KING TO A SECOND-PLACE FINISH AND THE CROWD GOES WILD.

LIGHTNING IS OFFERED THE DINOCO SPONSORSHIP! BUT LIGHTNING DECIDES TO STAY WITH THE LOYAL GUYS FROM RUST-EZE. HE DOES ASK DINOCO FOR ONE SMALL FAVOR, THOUGH: A HELICOPTER RIDE FOR HIS FRIEND MATER.

ALONE ON THE MOUNTAIN, SALLY IS LOOKING OUT OVER THE VALLEY WHEN LIGHTNING SURPRISES HER. HE SAYS HE'S OPENING UP HIS HEADQUARTERS IN TOWN. THEIR ROMANTIC MOMENT IS INTERRUPTED AS MATER APPEARS IN THE HELICOPTER, SINGING. SALLY LAUGHS AND TEARS OFF DOWN THE MOUNTAIN. MCQUEEN CHASES HER. THERE'S NOWHERE ELSE HE'D RATHER BE.

LIGHTNING MCQUEEN

LIGHTNING IS A HOTSHOT ROOKIE RACE CAR WHO CARES ONLY ABOUT TWO THINGS: WINNING AND THE FAME AND FORTUNE THAT COME WITH IT. BUT ALL THAT CHANGES WHEN HE SUDDENLY FINDS HIMSELF IN THE SLEEPY OLD TOWN OF RADIATOR SPRINGS.

STEP 1

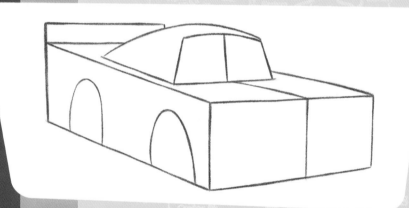

don't make pupils too big

NO!

YES!

STEP 2

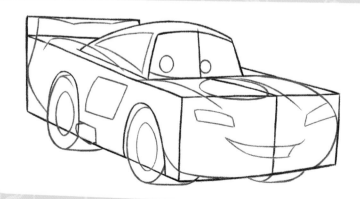

STEP 3

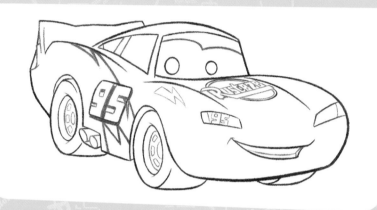

you can give Lightning different expressions by adjusting his eyelids

 sad

 curious

 intense

when Lightning looks down, don't bury eyes into body

NO!

YES!

STEP 4

MATER

MATER IS A FRIENDLY, ENTHUSIASTIC TOW TRUCK WITH A BIG HEART, WHO IS ALWAYS WILLING TO GIVE A HELPING HAND. HE IS THE SELF-PROCLAIMED WORLD'S BEST BACKWARDS DRIVER, AND HE ALSO GETS A KICK OUT OF TRACTOR TIPPING.

STEP 1

YES!

mirrors are at irregular angles

NO!

mirrors are not perfectly aligned

STEP 2

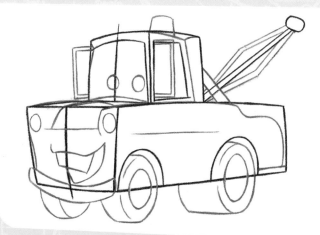

STEP 3

keep facial expressions off center to emphasize Mater's goofiness

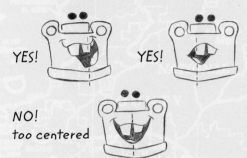

YES!

YES!

NO!
too centered

STEP 4

YES!

NO!

his misshapen buckteeth aren't perfect squares—and there's a gap between them

SALLY

SALLY, A SMART AND BEAUTIFUL SPORTS CAR, IS DETERMINED TO RESTORE RADIATOR SPRINGS TO THE BUSTLING TOWN IT WAS IN ITS HEYDAY. ORIGINALLY AN ATTORNEY FROM LOS ANGELES, SHE SHOWS LIGHTNING THAT SOMETIMES IT'S GOOD TO LIVE LIFE IN THE SLOW LANE.

STEP 1

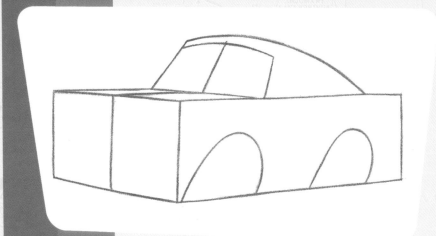

Sally's eyebrows are heaviest at the peaks

YES!

NO!

STEP 2

STEP 3

Sally is just about a tire width smaller than Lightning

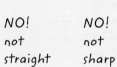

YES!
spokes
have
curved
pattern

NO!
not
straight

NO!
not
sharp

STEP 4

DOC HUDSON

Doc is a respected and admired town doctor, and he's the judge in Radiator Springs. But he has a mysterious past. Protective of the town, Doc cherishes the quiet and simple life. He wants nothing to do with the flashy race car Lightning.

STEP 1

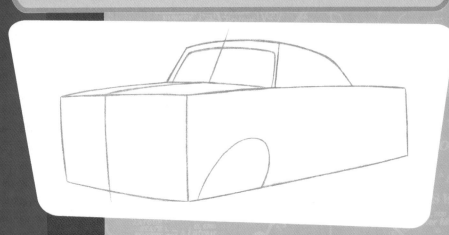

NO!

YES!

centerline helps transform
Doc's windshield into glasses

STEP 2

STEP 3

Doc's grille is like a rainbow built over the central letter A

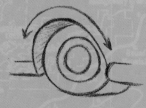

NO! front fender isn't round

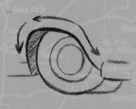

YES! fender curves into front bumper

STEP 4

Learn to Draw

Disney·Pixar
RATATOUILLE
(rat·a·too·ee)

Adapted by Howard Father and Claire Williams
Illustrated by The Disney Storybook Artists
Inspired by the character designs created by Pixar Animation Studios

Inside a cottage in the French countryside there lived a colony of rats. They kept to themselves in the attic of an old woman named Mabel.

One of the rats, Remy, possessed a highly developed sense of smell. He checked the rats' food from the old woman's compost heap to make sure it was safe to eat. But Remy had bigger dreams. He really wanted to be . . . a chef!

Remy's dad, Django, was proud of his son, the "food sniffer." But Django could not understand Remy's dreams about cooking food. So Remy kept his explorations in Mabel's kitchen a secret from everyone—except his brother Emile.

Emile didn't always understand his brother's odd behavior. And it made him very nervous when Remy started to read a cookbook written by his "favorite chef," Auguste Gusteau.

One day, as Remy and Emile sneaked into Mabel's kitchen for spices, Remy heard the TV announce that Gusteau had died. But before he could process the stunning news, the kitchen lights suddenly clicked on. Mabel had awakened! She nearly tore her whole house apart chasing after the rat brothers. Just as she had them trapped on the chandelier, the ceiling cracked and caved in—bringing the entire rat colony down with it! As Django led the rest of the rats to safety, Remy went back to get Gusteau's cookbook.

The rats jumped into their escape boats and headed down the river toward the sewer tunnels. Meanwhile, Remy escaped from Mabel's cottage and chased after his family. He used the cookbook as a raft and raced to catch up with the other rats, but he soon became lost in the tunnels of the sewer, all alone.

Then Remy heard a voice. It was Chef Gusteau, talking to him in his imagination! Gusteau told Remy to forget about the past; he encouraged Remy to leave the sewer and, instead, go up to the rooftop to see the sights. When Remy did what Gusteau suggested, he saw the beautiful night sky of Paris—and the bright sign of Gusteau's restaurant!

Remy peered through the skylight into the restaurant below. One of the cooks was introducing a tall, awkward young man named Linguini to Skinner, a tiny chef with an even tinier heart.

Linguini handed Skinner a sealed letter from his mother as he explained that he was looking for a job. Without reading the letter, Skinner reluctantly hired Linguini as the garbage boy. But as Linguini began his new job, he knocked over a pot of soup! He tried to cover his mistake by pouring water and spices into the pot to make more. Remy was so horrified at what he saw, he fell through the skylight. But as he ran to escape from the kitchen, he couldn't resist stopping and trying to fix the soup. He was busy adding a spice when Linguini caught sight of him.

Rat and human stared at each other in shock. But before Linguini could do anything, a waiter whisked away the soup to the hungry customers.

Skinner was furious at the idea that Linguini was cooking! He was going to fire Linguini but changed his mind when he discovered that the customers liked the soup. Linguini was saved, but Remy wasn't—when Skinner saw the rat, he ordered Linguini to take it away and kill it!

Remy found himself trapped in a jar because Linguini didn't have the heart to throw him into the river. When Linguini started talking to himself, he was surprised to see Remy

nod back. Linguini couldn't believe that the rat not only knew how to cook, but he also understood humans! Linguini took Remy to his apartment.

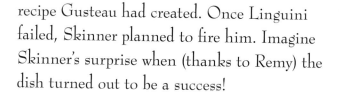

The next day, Skinner demanded that Linguini make his special soup again. Remy hid under Linguini's hat, tugging Linguini's hair this way and that way to "steer" him to the correct ingredients. Before long, Linguini was chopping, mixing, and pouring. They were a cooking team!

Meanwhile, Skinner opened the letter from Linguini's mother. The letter said that Linguini was Gusteau's son, but Linguini didn't know—and Gusteau hadn't known either! According to Gusteau's will, Skinner would own the restaurant if no heir was found—but this letter said Linguini was an heir. Skinner's lawyer told him not to worry—Skinner could keep an eye on Linguini while he investigated whether Linguini really was Gusteau's son.

Skinner hated the thought of Linguini owning the restaurant. So he set up Linguini and a chef named Colette to cook the only truly disastrous

recipe Gusteau had created. Once Linguini failed, Skinner planned to fire him. Imagine Skinner's surprise when (thanks to Remy) the dish turned out to be a success!

Outside the restaurant, Remy was happily eating the good food Linguini had shared with him, when he heard a noise. It was Emile! The brothers reunited, and Emile took Remy to the rat colony's new home in the sewers.

All the rats cheered when Remy arrived. But Remy wanted to return to the restaurant and his job. Django encouraged his son to stay in the sewer, explaining that the world belonged to humans, and that all humans were enemies to rats.

Meanwhile, Skinner's lawyer confirmed that Linguini was Gusteau's son and rightfully owned the restaurant. Skinner decided not to share the news. He intended to keep the restaurant; he just had to make sure that Linguini didn't discover he was Gusteau's heir.

Skinner's plan might have worked if Remy hadn't

discovered Gusteau's will—along with the letter from Linguini's mother. Remy grabbed the papers with his teeth and ran through the streets of Paris as Skinner chased after him. Remy ended up on a boat, Skinner in the river.

When Skinner returned to his office, soaking wet and furious, he found Linguini with his feet up on the desk. The jig was up! Linguini knew he rightfully owned the restaurant, and Skinner was fired.

But with the change, Linguini started paying more attention to his newfound fame than to his cooking. Remy didn't like it, and neither did Colette. Linguini had forgotten his friends.

After a bitter argument with Linguini, Remy decided enough was enough. He told Emile to gather the entire rat colony and bring them to the restaurant. When Linguini returned to apologize, he saw Remy and the rats stealing food from the walk-in refrigerator, so he kicked them all out!

The next day, Anton Ego, the famous restaurant critic, sat down at Gusteau's and requested whatever "Chef Linguini" dared to bring him. Skinner lurked nearby, smirking. He couldn't wait for Linguini to fail.

In the kitchen, Linguini explained to his staff that Remy—who had returned to help

Linguini—was really the cook, not him. But the chefs didn't want to work with a rat, so they all walked out. Linguini would have lost everything—if it weren't for the rats. Django had seen Linguini stand up for Remy, and he decided this human was not so bad. He told all the rats to help. They didn't know how to cook, but they did whatever Remy needed, and together they saved the day!

Colette also returned, and she helped Remy make a simple dish called "ratatouille," which Linguini served to Ego. Ego took a nibble. He loved it! The delicious ratatouille brought back memories of his mother's cooking. The food critic finished every morsel of the tasty meal.

When Skinner burst into the kitchen to find out just who had made the ratatouille, he faced a kitchen full of rats—who tied him up!

Meanwhile, Ego asked to meet the chef, and Linguini presented Remy to Ego. Ego was shocked, but he still gave the restaurant five stars. He even helped open a new bistro, La Ratatouille, with a very special chef in charge of the kitchen. Remy's dreams came true: the little rat had become a real chef in a real bistro in the heart of Paris!

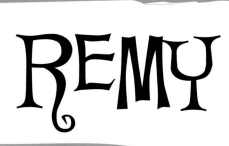
REMY

Remy is a little rat with big dreams. Born with a highly developed sense of smell, he can't stand eating garbage like the other rats, and he longs to become a gourmet chef. When Remy accidentally lands in the late, great Chef Auguste Gusteau's famous restaurant, Remy's dream just might come true . . . if he can remain hidden.

STEP 1

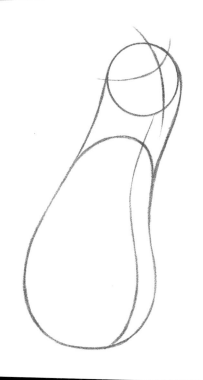

STEP 2

YES!
body leans
forward

NO!
doesn't tilt
backward

STEP 3

arm hair is ragged and loose

STEP 4

YES!
legs merge with body for a relaxed look

NO!
legs are not separate shapes

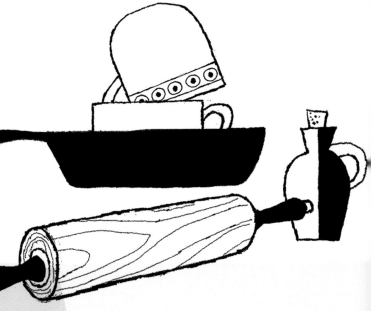

EMILE

Remy's younger brother Emile is a rat's rat. He loves life—especially food, edible or inedible! Emile's also a little overweight. He's always good-natured, and he's always there for his brother. Even though he doesn't understand Remy's passion for good food, Emile's bottomless appetite makes him the perfect taste-tester for Remy's culinary creations.

big body but thin, delicate wrists

STEP 1

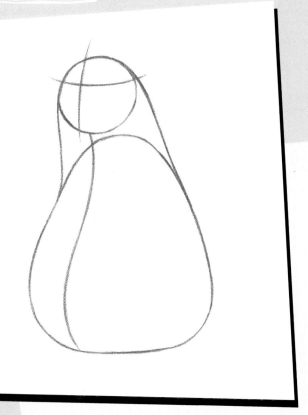

STEP 2

STEP 3

STEP 4

NO!
not large, high, and upright ears

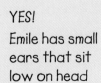

YES!
Emile has small ears that sit low on head

DJANGO

Remy's dad, Django, is the head of the rat colony. He is very proud that Remy is the group's "food sniffer," who makes sure their food is safe to eat. Django doesn't understand Remy's finicky tastes or his strange fascination with Gusteau's restaurant. To Django, humans are the enemy, and a restaurant kitchen is no place for a rat!

STEP 2

STEP 1

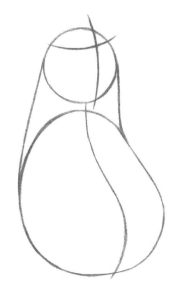

Django is much taller than his sons

eyebrows rest right on top of
eyes unless he is surprised

STEP 4

YES!
fingers are round
and smooth

NO!
not blocky and angular

61

LINGUINI & REMY

Linguini and Remy form an unusual partnership that takes them on harrowing adventures inside and out of Gusteau's restaurant. In the end, their hard work and strange working habits pay off deliciously!

STEP 2

STEP 1

Linguini's head is shaped like an upside-down egg

STEP 3

Linguini's chef hat

Linguini's garbage boy hat

STEP 4

63

LEARN TO DRAW

YOUR FAVORITE
Disney·PIXAR
CHARACTERS

Get ready to draw the best of the best from the blockbuster Disney/Pixar films!
From **Woody** and **Buzz** to **Sulley** and **Mike**
to **Mr. Incredible** and **Elastigirl,** this book is full of all your
favorite animated characters. And inside you'll find out
how to draw them all, just like the pros.
So grab some paper and sharpen your skills
(and your pencil)—then turn the page
to get started!

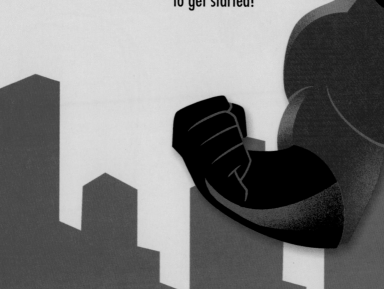

Buzz Lightyear

Buzz has stars in his eyes until Woody pulls him back down to earth. For most of *Toy Story*, Buzz doesn't understand that he's a toy. But in *Toy Story 2*, he understands so well that he has to remind Woody.

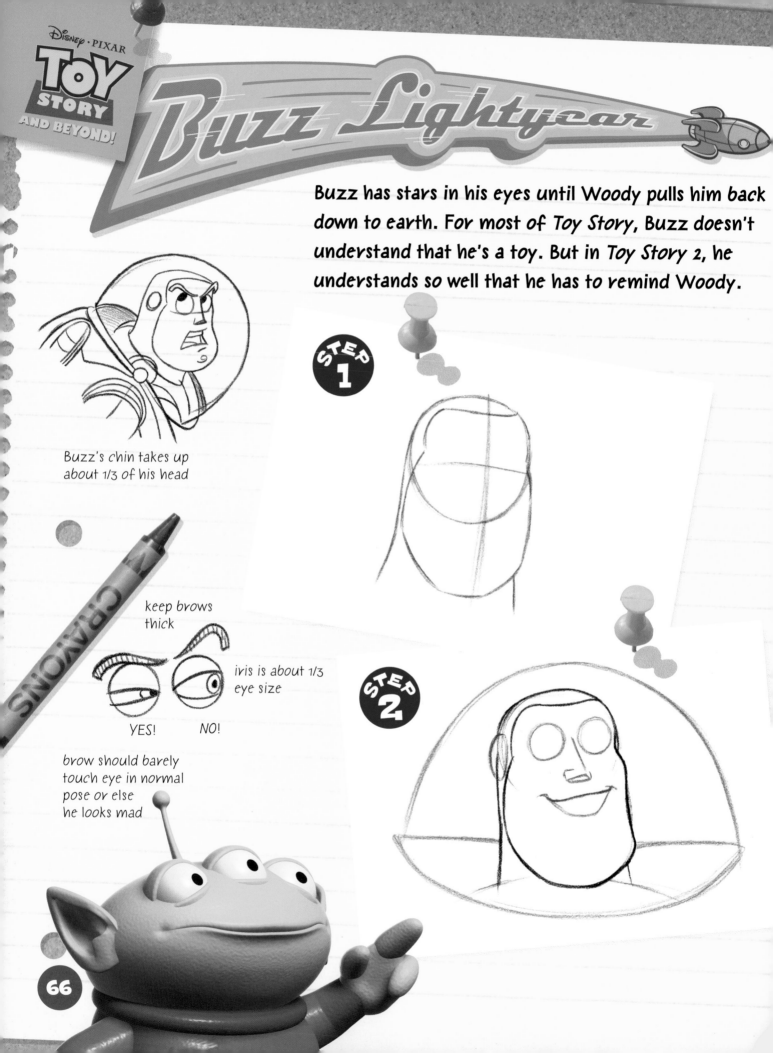

Buzz's chin takes up about 1/3 of his head

STEP 1

keep brows thick

iris is about 1/3 eye size

YES!   NO!

brow should barely touch eye in normal pose or else he looks mad

STEP 2

CRAYONS

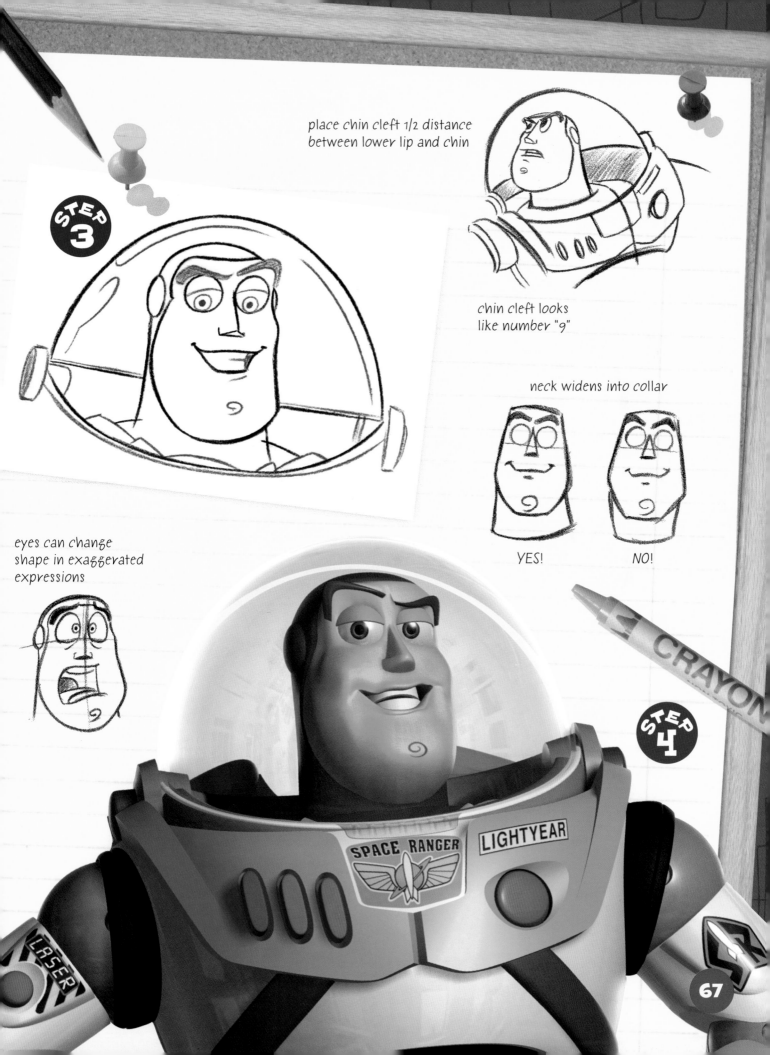

place chin cleft 1/2 distance between lower lip and chin

STEP 3

chin cleft looks like number "9"

neck widens into collar

YES!   NO!

eyes can change shape in exaggerated expressions

SPACE RANGER   LIGHTYEAR

STEP 4

CRAYON

LASER

WOODY

Woody is top toy in both *Toy Story* and *Toy Story 2*. That's a tough spot to share, especially with a new toy named Buzz Lightyear, who thinks he's a space ranger. But Woody takes it all in stride. After all, he's one tough cowboy. And he's smart enough to know that the best part about being a toy is having a special kid like Andy to play with.

CRAYONS

STEP 1

STEP 2

ears are flat on top

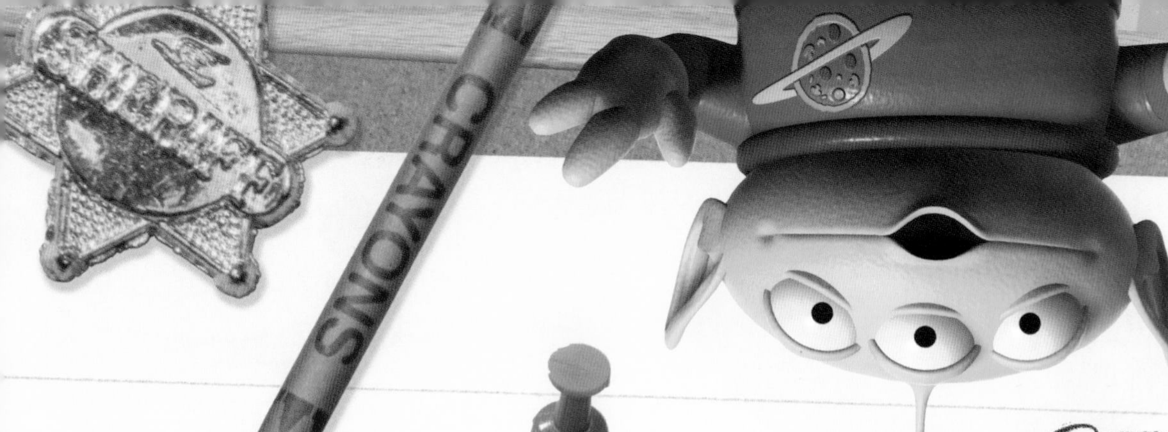

hair curl
is like the
letter "C"

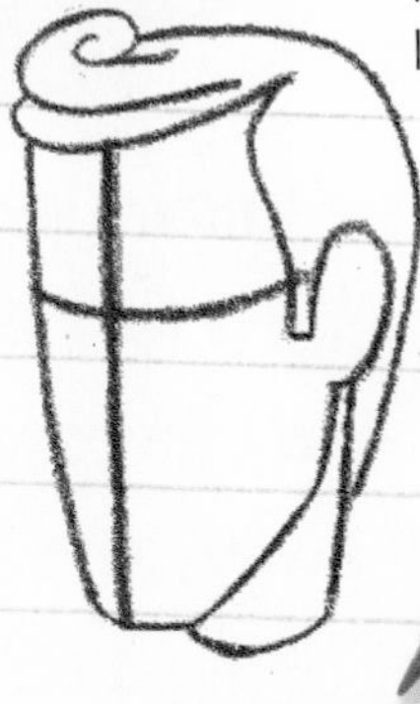

round eyes

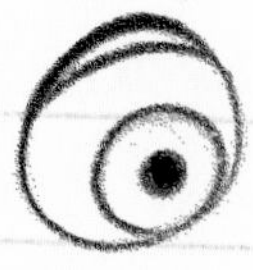

large iris
(1/2 of eye)

bottom half of head
shows off Woody's
handsome square
jawline

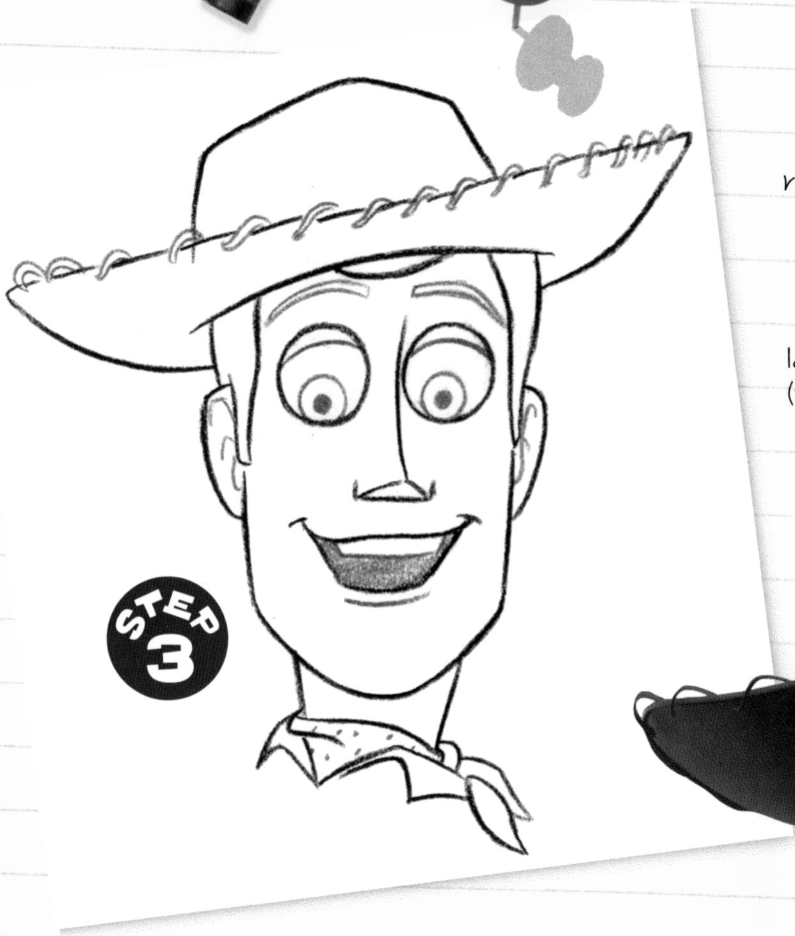

STEP 3

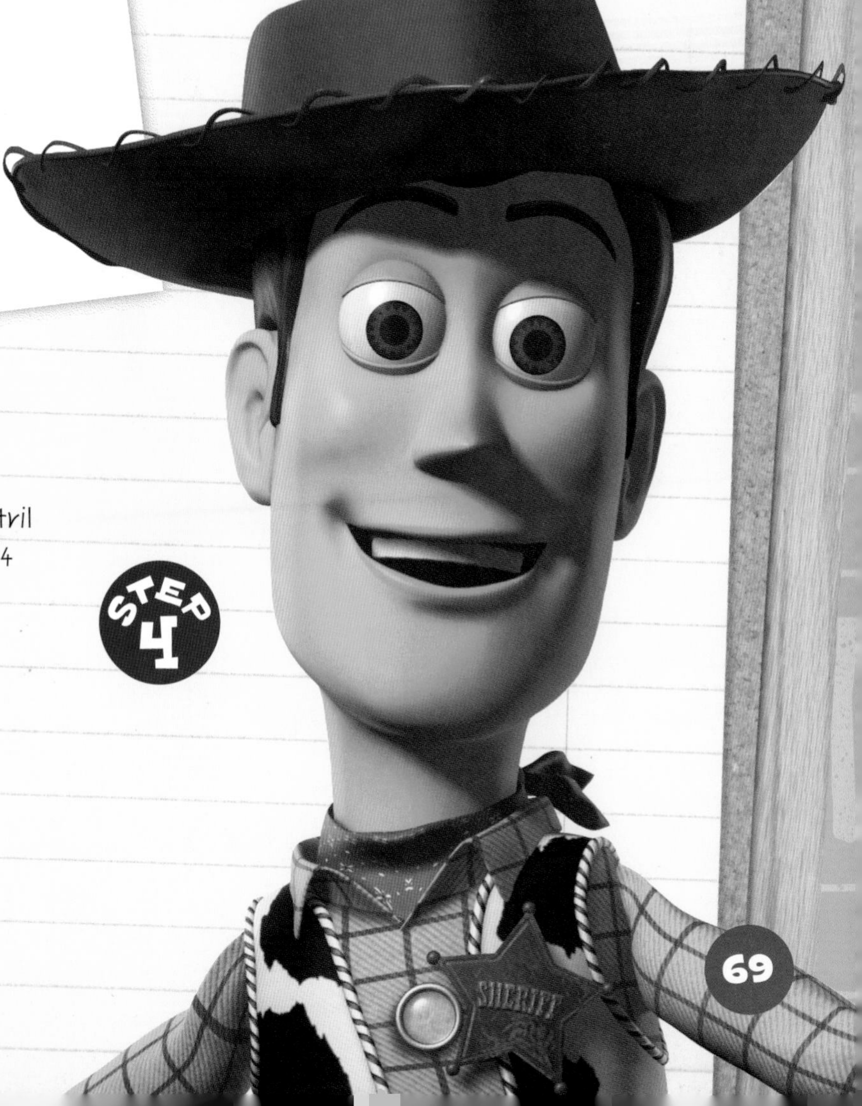

STEP 4

too
straight

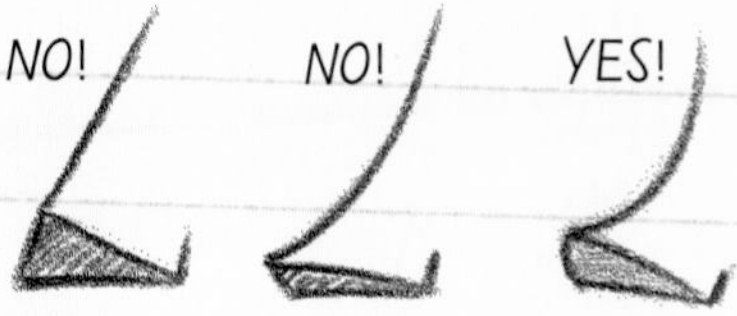

NO!   NO!   YES!   show nostril
side on 3/4
view or
profile

teeth are 1
long rectangle

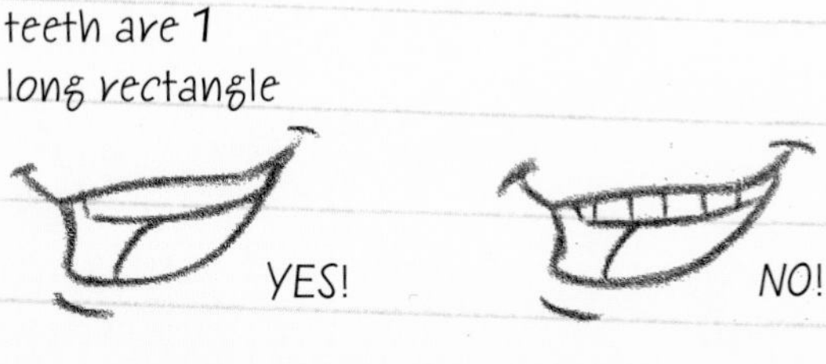

YES!   NO!

Jessie

Jessie knows what it means to be a toy. She once belonged to a little girl who loved her as much as Andy loves Woody. But that little girl gave her away, and the brokenhearted toy decided that being a collectible is better than being with a child who might outgrow you. Woody has to remind Jessie what being a toy is all about—and convince her to come back to Andy's room with him.

STEP 1

5 pieces of fringe attach to outside edge of chaps

chaps wrap around front of jeans

chaps looser on bottom to allow for boots

stitching wraps around cuff

shirt and gauntlet pattern

3 fringe pieces

YES!

NO!

she has a button nose

her hat usually sits on the back of her head

Woody's hat is triangular

Jessie's hat is rounder

pull-string on back

torso is shaped like a peanut

keep rag-doll body flexible

STEP 2

STEP 3

STEP 4

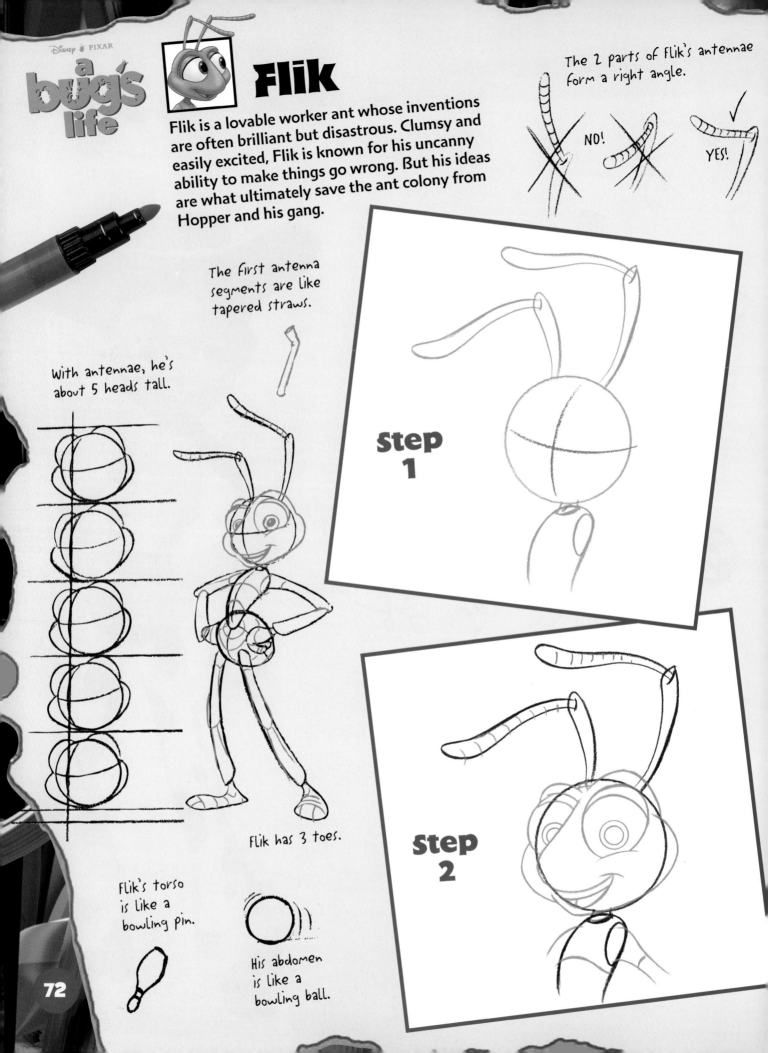

Disney · PIXAR
a bug's life

Flik

Flik is a lovable worker ant whose inventions are often brilliant but disastrous. Clumsy and easily excited, Flik is known for his uncanny ability to make things go wrong. But his ideas are what ultimately save the ant colony from Hopper and his gang.

The 2 parts of Flik's antennae form a right angle.

NO!   YES!

The first antenna segments are like tapered straws.

With antennae, he's about 5 heads tall.

Flik has 3 toes.

Flik's torso is like a bowling pin.

His abdomen is like a bowling ball.

Step 1

Step 2

Expressions

Sheepish

Choked up

Dismayed

A The pose is worked out with a stick figure.

B Then basic shapes are built up.

C Finally the details are added.

D Back to the drawing board!

The ants have 4 digits on each hand: 3 fingers and 1 thumb.

Flik's antennae are composed of 2 nearly straight segments.

Flik's arms look like sleeves.

step 3

A bit of eyelid usually shows.

His top teeth show when he smiles.

When Flik smiles, his cheek comes over the eye.

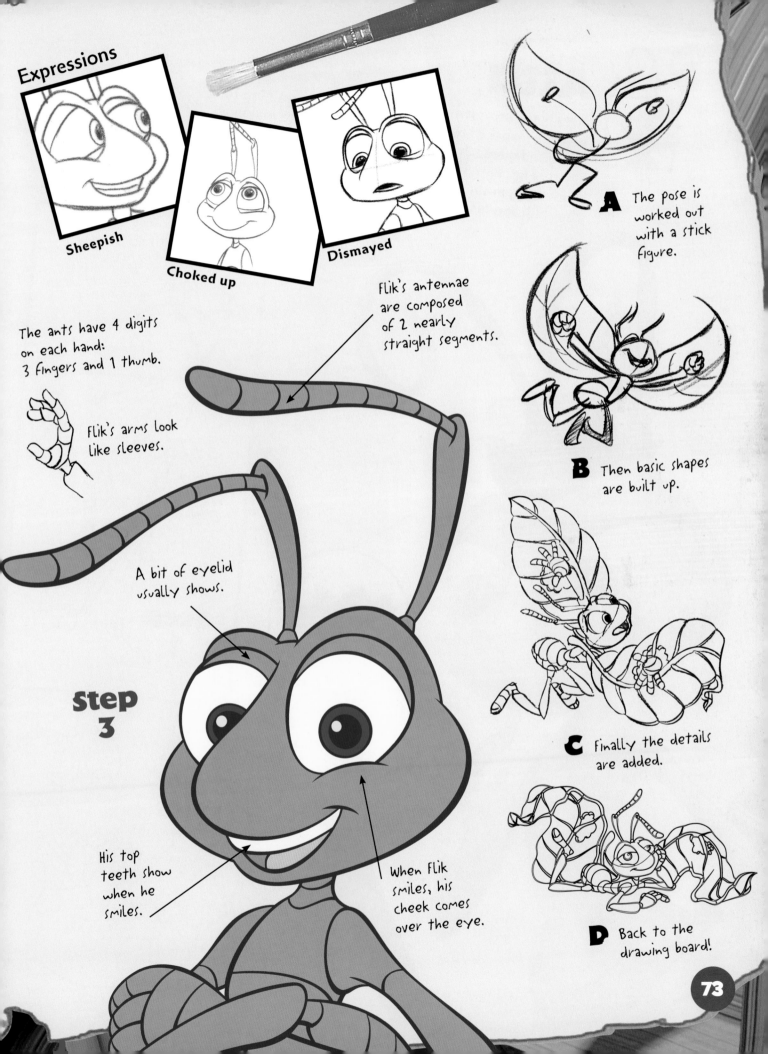

Atta

Atta is the stressed-out princess who is in training to become leader of the ant colony. She has the makings of a good queen, but she's still learning. Flik often flusters her with his unconventionality, but there is something in the back of Atta's mind that tells her that Flik and his ideas are worthy of consideration.

Atta's eyes are elliptical.

The tiara is made of leaves.

Atta's tiara has a jewel: a tiny drop of amber.

Step 1

She always has 3 long eyelashes.

The nose is pointy in profile.

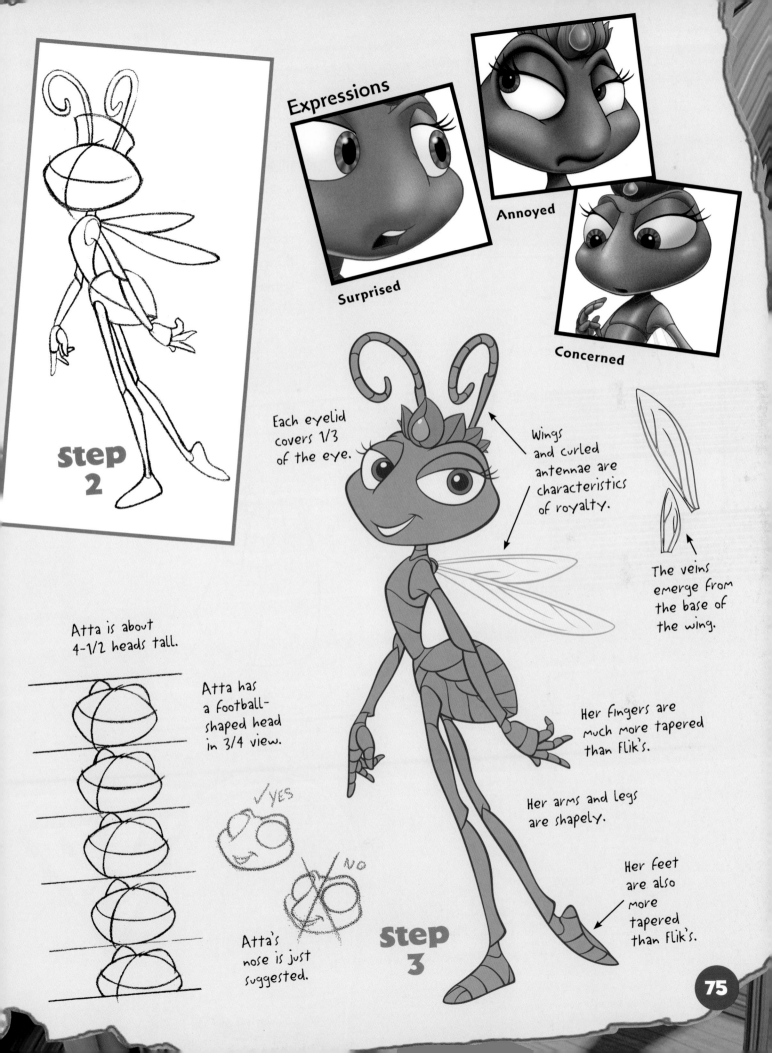

step 2

Expressions

Surprised

Annoyed

Concerned

Each eyelid covers 1/3 of the eye.

Wings and curled antennae are characteristics of royalty.

The veins emerge from the base of the wing.

Atta is about 4-1/2 heads tall.

Atta has a football-shaped head in 3/4 view.

✓ YES

✗ NO

Atta's nose is just suggested.

Her fingers are much more tapered than Flik's.

Her arms and legs are shapely.

Her feet are also more tapered than Flik's.

step 3

"RRROAR!" Although Sulley scares kids for a living, he really has a heart of gold and is an all-around nice guy. Sulley's a gentle giant who would never hurt anyone—especially not a kid! When he discovers that scaring them might not be the best thing for kids, he decides to do something about it, which changes Monsters, Inc., forever.

STEP 1

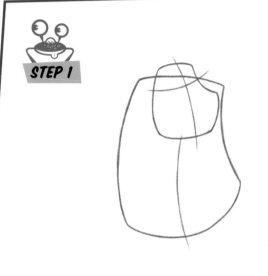

STEP 2

eyelid is rounded like this YES! NO!

YES! eyebrows overlap like this . . .

. . . and this

NO! not separated like this

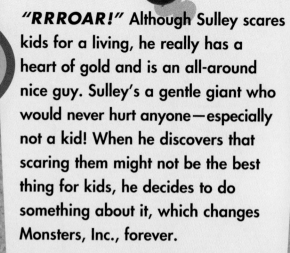

outside of horn has angles; inside is curved

WE SCARE BECAUSE WE CARE

SULLEY

YES! bend knees to show weight

NO! don't make legs too straight

STEP 4

STEP 3

STEP 5

draw big hands with pointed nails

don't round out toes

YES!   NO!

77

Mike

Both best friend and scare assistant to James P. Sullivan, Mike Wazowski is proud of his job, and he loves the perks that go along with it. Mike wouldn't change a thing about his life—except maybe to eliminate all the paperwork he has to do. A little green ball of energy, Mike is always ready with a joke and a smile, especially for his best girl, Celia.

STEP 1

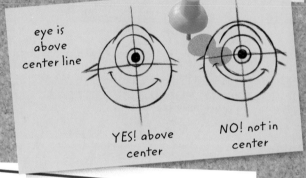

eye is above center line

YES! above center

NO! not in center

STEP 2

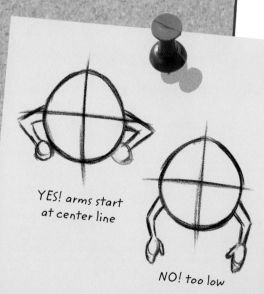

YES! arms start at center line

NO! too low

FOR YOUR SAFETY:

DO NOT FEED THE DISPATCHER

A man of super strength, Mr. Incredible was once the best-known, most popular Super alive! Then, through the Super Relocation Program, Mr. Incredible became "normal" Bob Parr, a claims adjuster at probably the worst insurance company ever. But Bob is not content with his ordinary life. He misses being a Super. One day, a mysterious summons calls the hero back to action. . . .

STEP 1

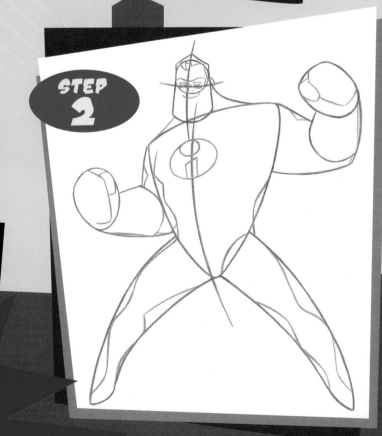

STEP 2

ELASTIGIRL

No one is as flexible as Elastigirl, a Super with an incredible reach! She could stretch her arm and land a punch before the crooks knew what hit them! But, as Helen Parr, Bob's wife and a mother of three, her Super powers are kept secret and largely unused—that is, until she finds out her Super spouse needs help! "Leave the saving of the world to the men? I don't think so!"

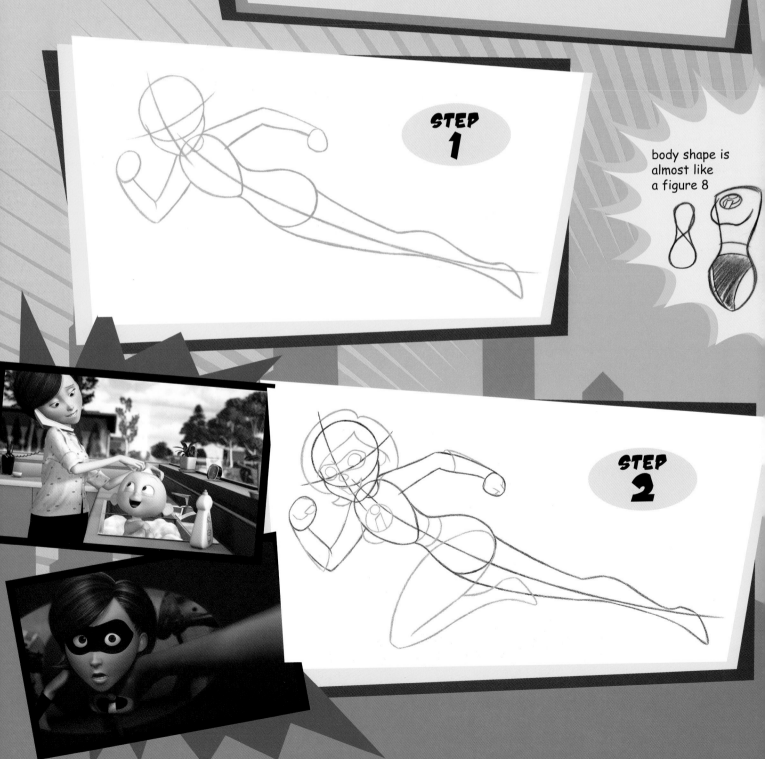

STEP 1

body shape is almost like a figure 8

STEP 2

STEP 3

STEP 4

STEP 5

keep
bridge of
nose short

YES!
short

NO!
not long

Helen's hair is
not completely
round—there
is a series of
flattened areas

FLAT

FLAT

FLAT

FLAT

LEARN TO DRAW

Illustrated by The Disney Storybook Artists
Inspired by the character designs created by Pixar Animation Studios

WALL·E

Imagine life in the twenty-ninth century on Earth—this is when our story begins. There are no humans on the planet in the year 2805. Earth is so polluted by trash

that all the people left centuries earlier to live in outer space. But this story is less about people than it is about one single trash-compacting robot: a Waste Allocation Load Lifter—Earth class, or WALL•E.

Tiny WALL•E was programmed to do one thing: collect and compact trash until humans could return to Earth

and live there once again. But WALL•E wanted to do more than clean up Earth—he wanted to find true love. And thanks to his great big robotic heart, he managed to change—and save—the entire universe.

For centuries, WALL•E lived alone on Earth with his pet cockroach. He gathered trash into his small chest cavity and compacted it into small cubes. Then he stacked the cubes into high towers—a slow but effective process of cleaning up Earth.

WALL•E had other interests too. One of his favorite things to do was to watch videos of old romantic movies; another was to search for interesting items to collect from the trash. This was unusual for a robot. WALL•E thought— and felt—outside of the job he was programmed to perform.

One day EVE—an Extraterrestrial Vegetation Evaluator—arrived. She was a sleek, modern, state-of-the-art robot. Twice WALL•E's size, EVE was egg shaped with a glossy white exterior and blue eyes. WALL•E fell in love at once.

But when EVE saw a little plant that WALL•E had found in the trash, she yanked it away from him and then instantly shut down. WALL•E could not wake her.

Soon after, a ship returned and took the sleeping EVE away. Without a second thought, WALL•E grabbed onto

the outside of the ship and went with her. He would follow her anywhere—and he did; right onto a huge luxury space liner called the *Axiom.*

The human passengers aboard the *Axiom* had devolved over the years, growing lazy because robots and other electronic devices met all of their needs and desires. WALL•E changed that. As he chased EVE throughout the giant ship, he accidentally set off a string of events that caused all of the passengers—enough to fill a small city—to open their eyes and become interested in life again.

It started when EVE was taken to the Captain's bridge. The Captain pushed a button, and she awoke—and delivered the plant! WALL•E was happy because he loved her. The Captain was happy because the plant

was proof that Earth could once again sustain life.

But the controller of the ship, Autopilot, had a different directive—he had been programmed to ensure that the *Axiom* never returned to Earth. EVE was determined to fight against Autopilot's directive—and WALL•E wanted to help her.

Eventually, everyone else on the ship joined the fight. The Captain was the first human to leave his hover chair and . . . WALK! Many others followed.

Robots overrode their directives and released the humans from their electronic surround systems. Free to think on their own, everyone saw that they needed to help WALL•E and EVE.

In the end, WALL•E sacrificed his little robotic body to help EVE complete her directive. But EVE's joy in allowing the *Axiom* to return to Earth was overcome by loss—she had fallen in love with WALL•E.

Luckily, robots can be repaired—and they can repair one another. Once back on Earth, EVE worked hard to save WALL•E. And soon he was his old self again—happy, innocent, and in love.

Eventually people returned to live on Earth. There was still a lot of work to do, but WALL•E had shown everyone that with a little gumption and a lot of heart, even a trash-bot can change the universe, making it a better place to live . . . and thrive.

WALL•E

WALL•E is a Waste Allocation Load Lifter—Earth class. Although considered a bit ancient for the twenty-ninth century, WALL•E is programmed with a strong directive: to collect and compact trash to clean up the overly polluted Earth. His boxy middle contains his compacting unit; his mechanical arms were designed to gather trash; and his triangular-shaped treads cover the wheels that help him maneuver over the rugged, trash-covered terrain.

YES!
eyes stay in middle
of face

NO!
they don't move
around on head

Step 1

Step 2

Step 3

Step 4

WALL·E's treads change
shape when he moves

normal

high-speed

tip-toes

EVE

EVE is a probe-bot—an Extraterrestrial Vegetation Evaluator.
That means she was programmed with the directive to find
vegetation on Earth. If she finds a single plant on Earth,
humans can return from their space travels and live on
Earth again. A growing plant means the Earth's polluted
environment can once again sustain life!

facial expressions

neutral

worried or sad

skeptical

laughing

Step 1

Step 2

chest
compartment
can open

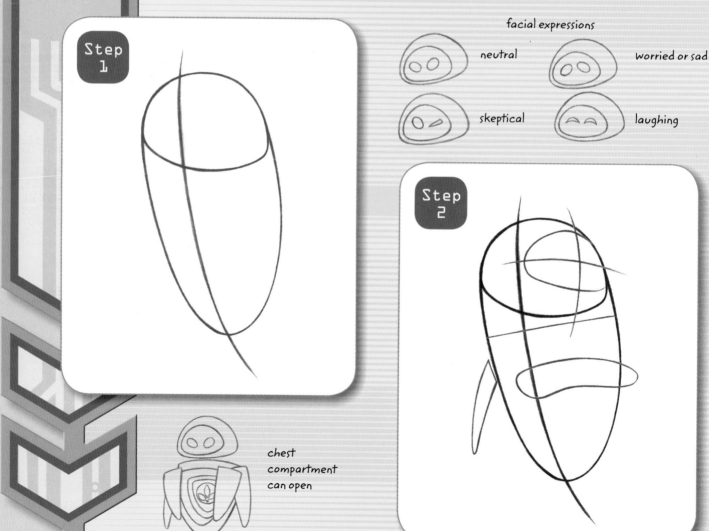

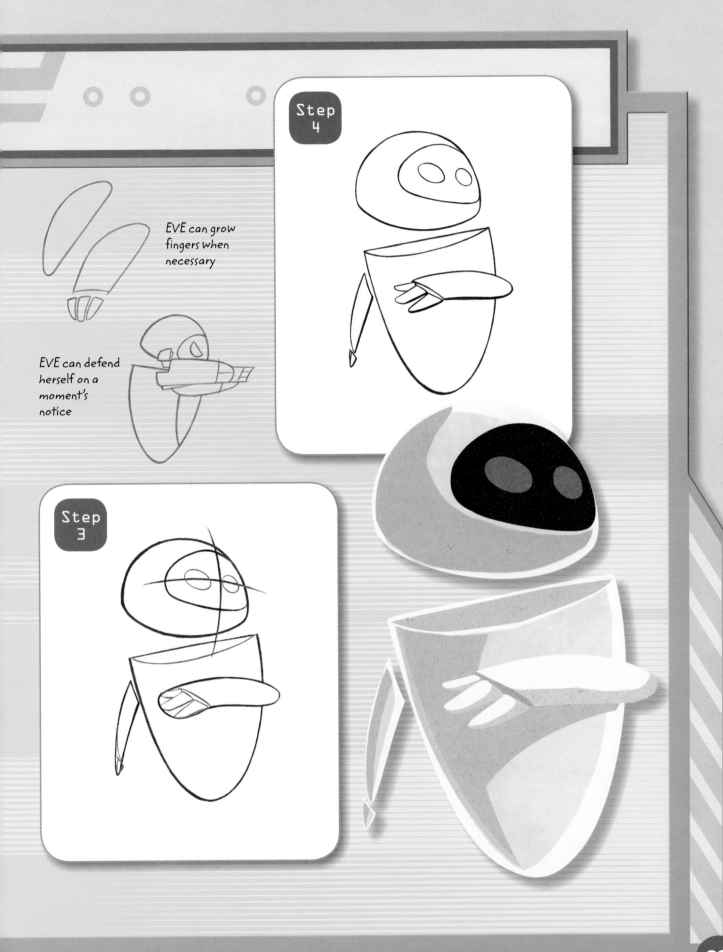

EVE can grow fingers when necessary

EVE can defend herself on a moment's notice

Step 4

Step 3

AUTOPILOT

The ship's autopilot, nicknamed Auto, has complete control over the ship. Shaped like a ship's wheel with a large eye in its center, Auto is attached to a long, electronic neck device that allows him to maneuver around the ship's bridge. He steers the ship and looks out the windows into space with his big eye, but he's not as innocent as he seems. When his true directive is discovered, he uses his robotic "finger" device not only to push buttons but also to poke the Captain in the eye!

Autopilot resembles an old ship's wheel

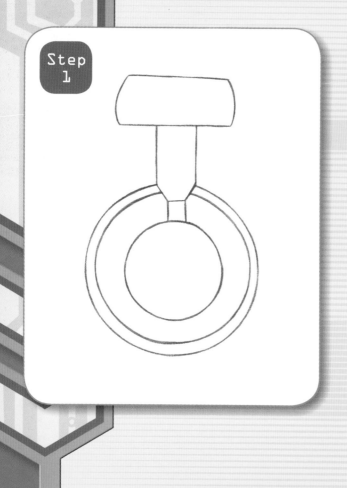

Step 1

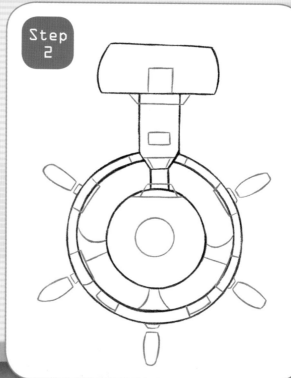

Step 2

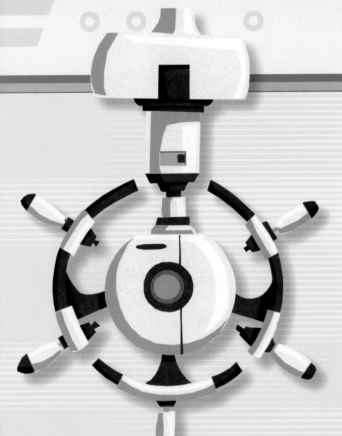

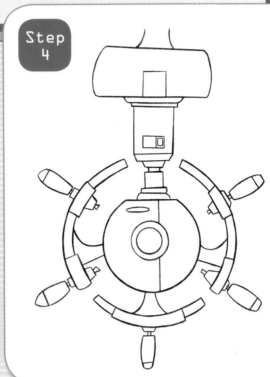

Step 4

Step 3

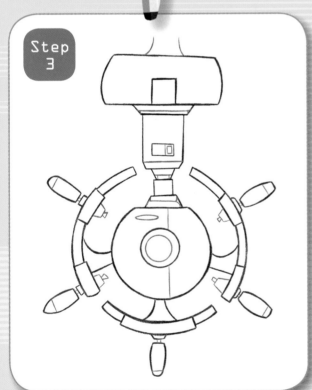

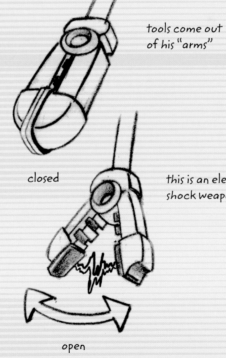

tools come out of his "arms"

closed

this is an electro-shock weapon

open

GO-4

light inside head flashes in an emergency

GO-4 is a robot that is supposed to serve the Captain and Auto, all for the good of the ship and its passengers. But once Auto is given his secret directive (never to steer the *Axiom* back to Earth), GO-4 becomes Auto's minion. With a siren on his head, GO-4 doesn't hesitate to declare an emergency to try to stop WALL•E and EVE—or anyone else who might try to help send the *Axiom* back to Earth.

Step 1

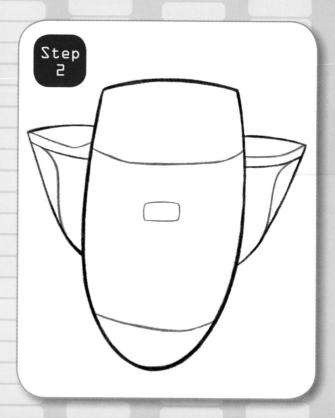

Step 2

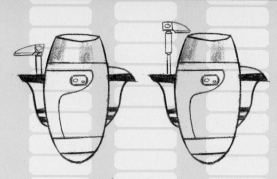

arms come up from side so he can salute

body is shaped like a football with one end cut off

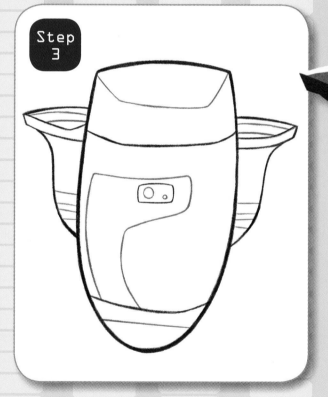

Learn to Draw

Disney · Pixar

FINDING NEMO

Adapted by
Nancy Parent

Illustrated
by the Disney
Storybook
Artists

Walter Foster

The Story of

Hi! My name is Marlin—you know, Nemo's father. I'm here to tell you a story. It's all about finding my son . . . finding Nemo. Years ago, Coral, my dear wife, and I were watching over our hundreds of eggs in our new home at the Drop-off. Suddenly, a barracuda attacked, and Coral and all the eggs were taken from me. I was devastated.

Then I saw one tiny damaged egg left. I named the newborn Nemo and promised I would never let anything happen to him.

Nemo is a great little guy, despite the fact that when he was younger he was much too curious and adventurous for an overprotective father like me. He was born with one damaged fin, which I called his "lucky" fin. Unfortunately this lucky fin kept him from being a great swimmer. And that made me worry even more.

I kept Nemo out of school for as long as I could, but I finally had to give in. After all, I couldn't send a teenager off to first grade! On the first day of school, I thought I would be okay until I learned that their first field trip was going to the dangerous Drop-off! I raced after the class and found Nemo at the edge of the deep water!

I admit I panicked. I embarrassed poor Nemo so much that he felt he had to prove he was brave and strong. Before I knew it, he was swimming out to the deep water. He tagged a boat, impressing his new school friends. But then something terrible happened: A scuba diver swam up behind my son and netted him!

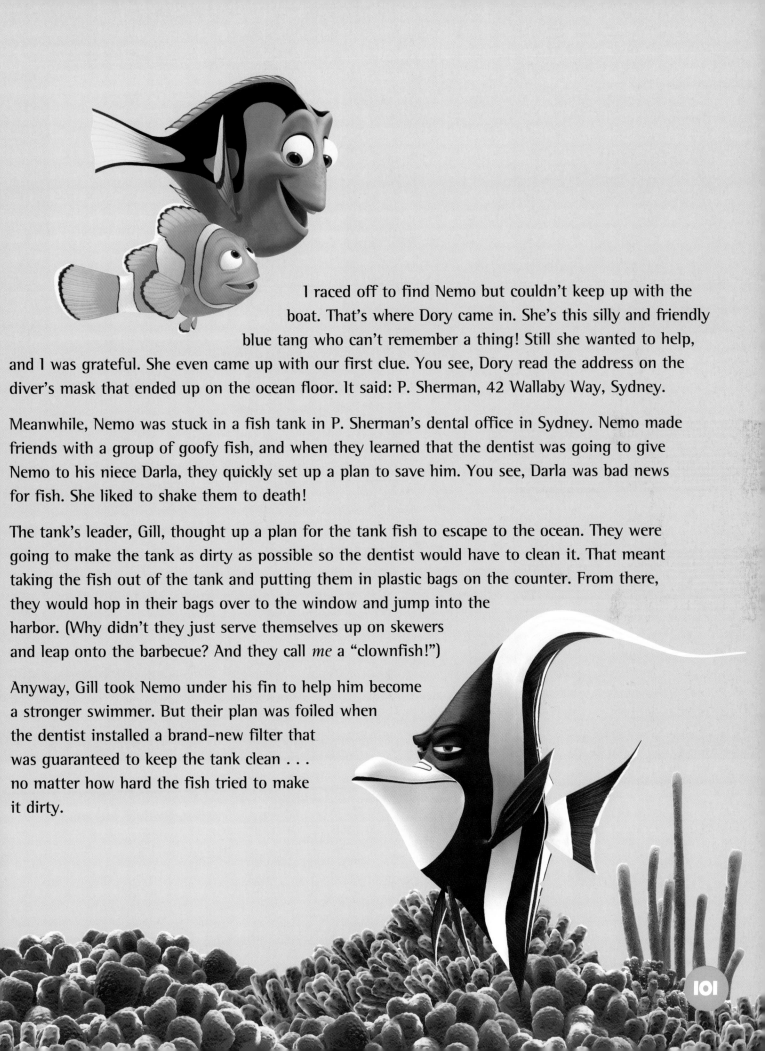

I raced off to find Nemo but couldn't keep up with the boat. That's where Dory came in. She's this silly and friendly blue tang who can't remember a thing! Still she wanted to help, and I was grateful. She even came up with our first clue. You see, Dory read the address on the diver's mask that ended up on the ocean floor. It said: P. Sherman, 42 Wallaby Way, Sydney.

Meanwhile, Nemo was stuck in a fish tank in P. Sherman's dental office in Sydney. Nemo made friends with a group of goofy fish, and when they learned that the dentist was going to give Nemo to his niece Darla, they quickly set up a plan to save him. You see, Darla was bad news for fish. She liked to shake them to death!

The tank's leader, Gill, thought up a plan for the tank fish to escape to the ocean. They were going to make the tank as dirty as possible so the dentist would have to clean it. That meant taking the fish out of the tank and putting them in plastic bags on the counter. From there, they would hop in their bags over to the window and jump into the harbor. (Why didn't they just serve themselves up on skewers and leap onto the barbecue? And they call *me* a "clownfish!")

Anyway, Gill took Nemo under his fin to help him become a stronger swimmer. But their plan was foiled when the dentist installed a brand-new filter that was guaranteed to keep the tank clean . . . no matter how hard the fish tried to make it dirty.

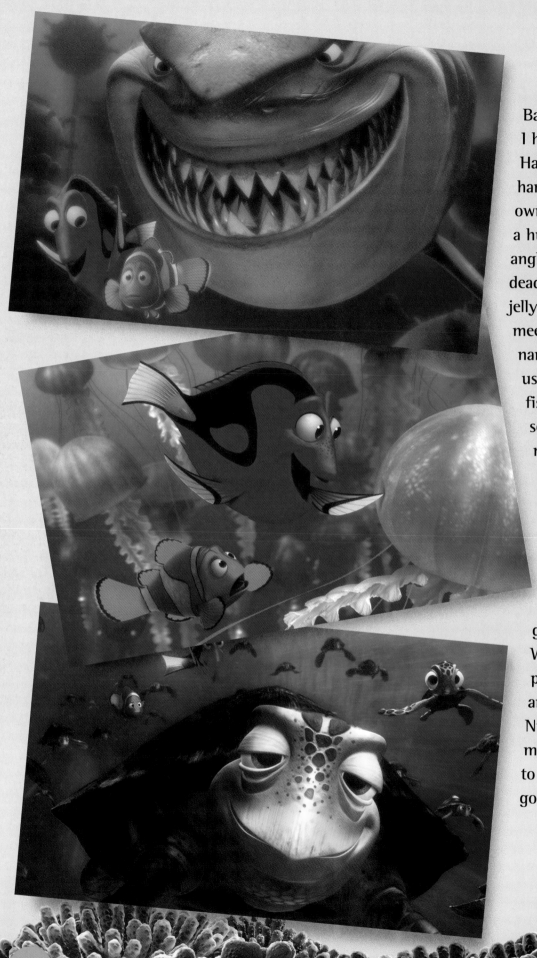

Back in the ocean, Dory and I had finally reached Sydney Harbor after some pretty harrowing adventures of our own—including run-ins with a hungry shark, a vicious anglerfish, and an almost-deadly forest of stinging jellyfish. The best part was meeting this cool turtle named "Crush" who rescued us after we escaped the jellyfish. He had the cutest little son named "Squirt" who reminded me of Nemo.

Then, when we got to the harbor, a pelican tried to eat us for breakfast! But I figured I had traveled so far to find Nemo that I wasn't about to give up. I fought like crazy. We were coughed up and picked up off the dock by another pelican named Nigel. Somehow he knew my story and took us right to the dentist's office. I was going to find my son!

Little did we know that Darla had arrived, ready for her present. The dentist scooped Nemo into a little plastic bag. But Nemo tricked the guy by playing dead. The tank fish realized Nemo was trying the "toilet escape"—he would get flushed down the toilet and make his way to the ocean. The fish were ecstatic . . . until the dentist headed for the trash can!

When Dory, Nigel, and I got there, I saw Nemo, looking dead as could be, floating in that little plastic bag. I was overcome with grief. I had no idea the little guy was actually still alive! The dentist pushed Nigel out the window, and the friendly pelican took Dory and me back to the harbor.

Meanwhile, the tank fish launched Gill out of the tank to save Nemo. He hit a dental mirror that Nemo was resting on and sent Nemo flying into the spit sink and down the drain into the harbor!

Minutes later, Dory ran into Nemo in the harbor. I had already left Dory because I was so sad that I wanted to be alone. It took her a little while to recognize Nemo, but when she did, they raced off together until they found me! But then a huge fishing net came down and trapped a bunch of fish, including Dory! Nemo got an idea. If the fish "swam down," they could pull on the net and break free. Nemo wanted to get into the net with the doomed fish to help them! I was beside myself—I had finally found my son, and now he wanted to risk his life! Well I finally let him go, and it worked! The fish were freed, and Nemo and I shared a really happy reunion. Dory joined right in.

When Dory, Nemo, and I made our way home to the reef, Nemo was excited about going back to school. And this time, I was ready to let him go.

Oh, and by the way, last I heard, Nemo's tank friends were floating in little plastic bags in the harbor. Seems Gill's escape plan finally worked. . . .

Nemo

Clownfish

You remember Nemo. He's my son— the adventurous little fish with the "lucky" fin who longs for excitement and friends to play with. But instead, he's saddled with me, an overprotective single dad who never lets the poor little guy out of sight.

Well, one day, Nemo dares to show his friends he's not scared of the ocean (the way his dad is), and he swims off alone. He ends up getting a lot more excitement than he bargained for! But he also discovers just how brave and resourceful he can be. That's my boy!

from side, Nemo is shaped like Goldfish® cracker

from front, body looks like gumdrop

"lucky" fin is wedge-shaped with notch cut out

YES! rays follow curve of fin

NO! too straight and even

YES! varied stripe shapes

NO! too similar and too straight

YES! top (dorsal) fin is 2 different shapes pointing at different angles

NO! too even; too upright

3

4

5

top fin is same height as 1 eye

Nemo is about 4 "eyes tall" including top fin

4
3
2
1
0

YES! bottom fins are set apart from each other

NO! fins don't look like bow tie

105

Marlin

Clownfish

I'm that not-so-funny clownfish, Marlin (Nemo's dad). After losing almost all my family, I sort of become crazy about doing everything possible to keep my only son safe from the dangerous ocean. Unfortunately, I go a little overboard and don't allow Nemo to do anything—I don't even let him go to school!

I fuss and fret a lot, but I really do mean well. It takes a little journey across the ocean, and meeting up with Dory, to teach me the meaning of trust and letting go. When it comes down to it, I'm just a regular dad who will do anything for his son.

Marlin is about 2 times the size of Nemo

rays on Marlin's fins and tail radiate out from "meaty" parts of body like this . . .

"meaty" parts

. . . not like this

face is kind of flat

5 rays on side (pectoral) fins and tail

4

from side, shaped like turkey drumstick

3

bags under eyes make him look tired

YES! eyes close together

NO! eyes too far apart

5

Dory

Regal Blue Tang

Dory is one chatty, friendly, funny fish! She never gives up hope—when things get tough, she just keeps on swimming. Always willing and helpful, Dory has everything going for her except for one small thing—her memory. She can't remember anything! But she risks her own life to help me find Nemo (despite the fact that she can't remember the little guy's name!).

1

from front, Dory's stripe defines where "eyebrows" end

freckles follow curved bridge of "nose"

YES! curved freckle pattern

NO! too straight

2

Dory is just over 4 times the size of Nemo

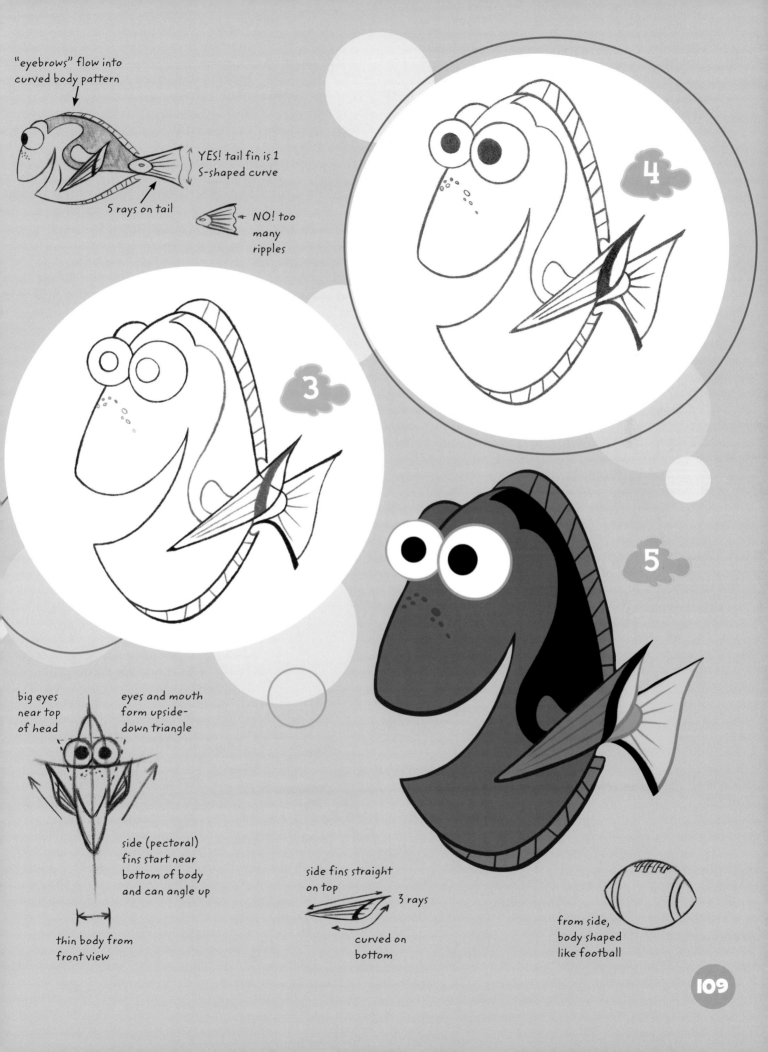

"eyebrows" flow into curved body pattern

YES! tail fin is 1 S-shaped curve

5 rays on tail

NO! too many ripples

4

3

5

big eyes near top of head

eyes and mouth form upside-down triangle

side (pectoral) fins start near bottom of body and can angle up

thin body from front view

side fins straight on top

3 rays

curved on bottom

from side, body shaped like football

Gill

Moorish Idol

Gill is the leader of the tank fish—a group of fish trapped in a tank in a dentist's office. According to Nemo, Gill is charming, likable, tough, and determined to break his friends out of the tank. He takes Nemo under his "scarred" fin to teach him the ropes and gives Nemo a part to play in the great escape he's been planning for years. Gill is a dreamer, a believer, and a doer, and I'll always be grateful to him.

YES! big, blocky eyebrows

eyes usually half closed

one line under each eye

NO! brows are too thin

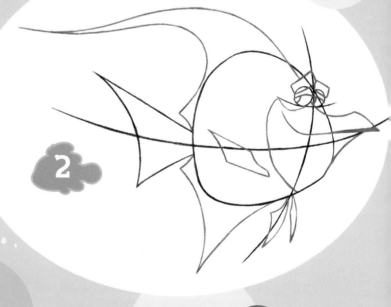

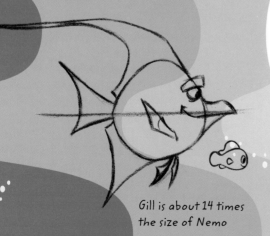

Gill is about 14 times the size of Nemo

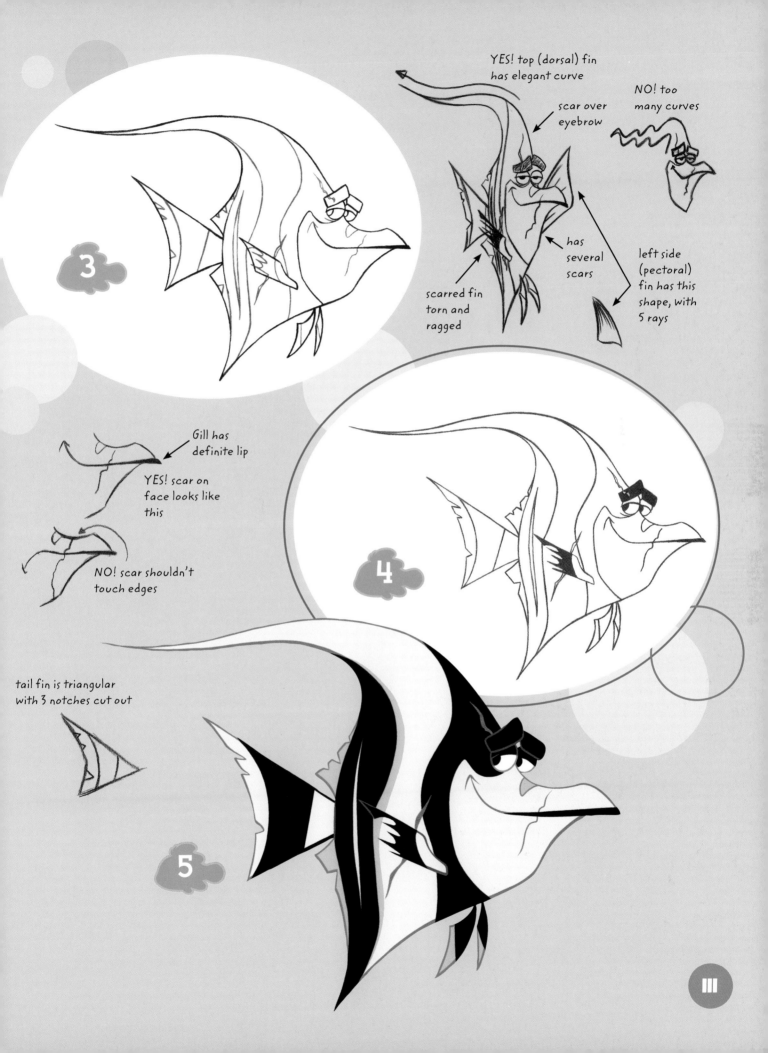

3

YES! top (dorsal) fin has elegant curve

NO! too many curves

scar over eyebrow

has several scars

scarred fin torn and ragged

left side (pectoral) fin has this shape, with 5 rays

Gill has definite lip

YES! scar on face looks like this

NO! scar shouldn't touch edges

4

tail fin is triangular with 3 notches cut out

5

Learn to Draw

Illustrated by the Disney Creative
Development Storybook Art Staff under the
guidance of Walt Disney Feature Animation

Written by Annie Auerbach and Lori Heiss

The name, image, and likeness of Elvis Presley
are used courtesy of Elvis Presley Enterprises, Inc.

An Introduction from Lilo & Stitch Writer/Director Chris Sanders

Lilo & Stitch marks an artistic return to the rounded characters and watercolor backgrounds of the 1940s, as well as a return to the storytelling style that first defined the heart and soul of Disney studios. As with **Bambi** and **Dumbo,** a powerful and unflinching story lies beneath the film's friendly exterior.

We produced **Lilo & Stitch** entirely at our feature animation branch in Orlando, Florida. I found the studio, with its young, enthusiastic artists, to be a great place for developing new ideas—many of which you'll discover as you learn to draw the characters from Lilo's world.

Lilo & Stitch was a bold move for a studio that had been used to working with an angular animation style. These characters and backgrounds are based on circular rather than angled shapes. This can make drawing them challenging, but as artists who also had to learn to draw these characters, we give you plenty of clues about how to construct them and what to avoid. So keep practicing: Drawing this group is a lot of fun!

One of the curious things about drawing characters is that the more extreme they are, the easier they are to draw! That's because you don't notice if the lines aren't quite exact when the characters have big, exaggerated features. I recommend starting with Stitch because his design is easily the most extreme in Lilo's world. (Besides . . . who could be more fun?) Happy drawing!

Chris Sanders

The Story of
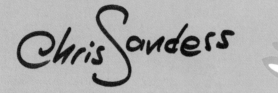

In a far-off galaxy, the Intergalactic Council had come together to save the universe from a small but dangerous creature—Experiment 626. Created by a rebel scientist named Jumba Jukiba, 626 was an indestructible fighting machine, programmed to destroy everything in his path. Governed by the Grand Councilwoman, the committee decided that Jumba and his evil experiment should be jailed.

Experiment 626 was sent away on a transport ship belonging to a giant alien named Captain Gantu, who was no match for the devilish smarts of 626. He freed himself from his captors, escaped in a little red police spaceship, and launched himself into dangerous territory—the far reaches of space. The Grand Councilwoman was furious when she heard that 626 was on a direct course for Quadrant 17, Section 005, Area 51 . . . a place the aliens called "E-aaarth." It was Earth! She wanted to destroy the far-off planet, but was stopped by Agent Pleakley, who considered himself an expert on Earth. Pleakley really just had an old toy from Earth called a View-Master, but he was able to convince the Grand Councilwoman to spare the strange planet. To get 626 back, the Grand Councilwoman promised Jumba his freedom if he could find and capture his invention on Earth, and she sent Pleakley to keep his eye on him.

Meanwhile on Earth, a happy little girl named Lilo swam in the Hawaiian waters near her home before rushing off to hula school. Lilo and her older sister Nani had been living by themselves since their parents had died. After a bad day at school, Lilo was lying on the floor, cheering herself up by listening to music. But she had nailed the door shut, leaving Nani stuck outside! And this was no ordinary day; this was the day a new social worker was coming to check on them. If everything wasn't perfect, Lilo could be sent to a foster home. They *had* to make a good impression!

Cobra Bubbles, the social worker, arrived before Nani could get into the house—and the place was a mess! Even worse, it was obvious that Lilo had been left alone. No matter how hard they tried, the girls could not convince Cobra that they could take care of each other. Cobra warned Nani: She had three days to change his mind.

That night, a shooting star streaked across the sky and Lilo made a wish—for someone to be her friend. Nani overheard her sister's wish and wanted to make it come true. So the next day, the sisters went to the animal rescue center, and Lilo picked out a strange looking . . . *puppy?* But she hadn't chosen a puppy at all—it was Experiment 626! To hide from Jumba and Pleakley, 626 had disguised himself to look like the other dogs by sucking in his extra legs, spikes, and antennae. Naming her new friend "Stitch," Lilo took him home—over Nani's strong objections.

Lilo and Stitch quickly became best friends. They did everything together. And "everything" included getting Nani fired from her job! Nani told Lilo that Stitch would have to go back to the shelter. But Lilo loved Stitch; he was part of their family now. She reminded Nani of the Hawaiian tradition of family, 'ohana: Nobody gets left behind or forgotten. Nani reluctantly agreed that Stitch could stay, at least for now. . . .

When Cobra visited Nani and Lilo again, Stitch threw a book at his head. Losing patience with the little family, Cobra told Nani that she had to get a job and that Lilo had to teach Stitch to behave. Nani interviewed for jobs, but Lilo and Stitch ruined every one of them! Time was running out.

To cheer themselves up, the sisters went surfing with Nani's friend David. But more trouble was afoot: Jumba and Pleakley turned up under the waves to capture Stitch. In the struggle, Stitch dragged Lilo underwater! Although David and Nani rescued them, all was not well; Cobra saw the whole thing! He thought that it was time to separate the sisters, and Stitch knew that it was his fault. He left and hid in the woods.

Angry that Jumba and Pleakley had failed to capture 626, the Grand Councilwoman fired them and sent Captain Gantu to replace them. But Jumba—still determined to capture Stitch—found him in the woods and chased him all the way back to Lilo's house. Lilo called the only person she could think of to help her—Cobra!

But it was too late—Jumba had blown up Lilo's house! Lilo ran into the woods, where she found Stitch in his true alien form. She was furious when she realized that Stitch wasn't a puppy, but in the middle of her outburst, Gantu leaped out of some nearby bushes, captured them, and loaded them into his spaceship. Stitch managed to escape and tried to save Lilo, but he was knocked off the ship as it took off— with Lilo still on board!

By explaining what he'd learned about 'ohana, Stitch convinced Nani that he could help her. Then he got Jumba and Pleakley to help rescue Lilo. They caught up with Gantu and collided with his ship, giving Stitch a chance to jump on board and save Lilo. But he was bounced back to Earth! Thankfully, Stitch was built to be indestructible *and* clever. By blowing up an oil tanker, Stitch blasted himself through Gantu's windshield and right onto his lap. Finally, Stitch managed to crash-land on the wing of Jumba's ship. He had saved Lilo!

When they landed back on the beach in Hawaii, the Grand Councilwoman was waiting for them . . . with handcuffs. But Lilo convinced her to let Stitch stay with them by explaining that Stitch was part of her family now. She proved that she owned him by showing the paperwork from the animal rescue center. The Grand Councilwoman took off with Gantu, leaving Jumba, Pleakley, and Stitch to live on Earth.

Lilo was able to keep living with her sister, and she also had some new family members—Jumba, Pleakley, Cobra, David, Nani, and Stitch. This family truly embodied the tradition of 'ohana: None of them were left behind, and none of them would ever be forgotten— especially Stitch!

Stitch

Stitch is truly one-of-a-kind—an alien experiment gone wrong. Although he can make himself look like a harmless puppy dog, Stitch is actually programmed to destroy! It's only when he becomes part of Lilo's family that he's able to overcome his destructive tendencies.

STEP 1

STEP 2

top of nose is higher than eyes

eye corners fall just below midsection of nose

eyebrows and eyelids follow teardrop shape of eyes

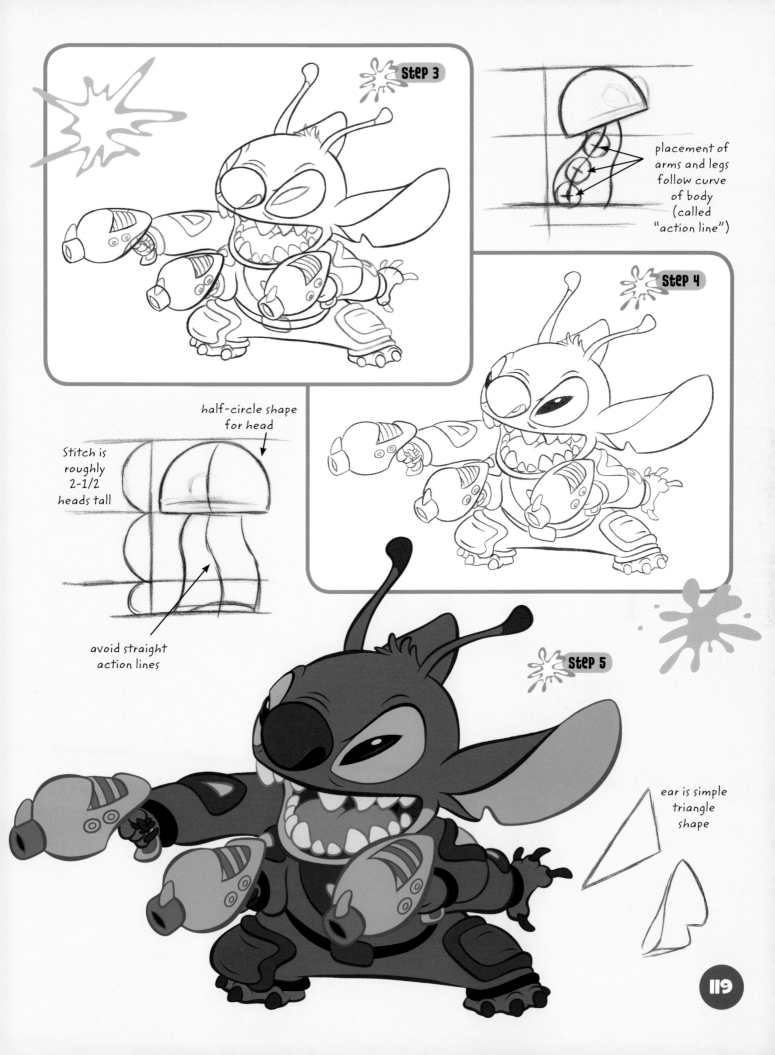

STEP 3

placement of arms and legs follow curve of body (called "action line")

STEP 4

half-circle shape for head

Stitch is roughly 2-1/2 heads tall

avoid straight action lines

STEP 5

ear is simple triangle shape

119

in profile, nose is large and round

from front, nose appears wide and flat

STEP 1

Only 5 years old, Lilo is an adorable and cheerful little girl. She is extremely imaginative and loves all things odd! Lilo is spirited, feisty, and determined. But it's not always easy being different. Lilo desperately wants to find a friend who won't leave her.

STEP 2

HANDS

YES!
fingers are short and stubby

NO!
not long and thin

round, chubby
forearm is same
size as hand

step 3

step 4

step 5

rounded tip
of nose ends
just below
eye line

eye line

YES! just
below eye line

NO! not above
eye line

Lilo & Stitch

Although they have a strange relationship, Lilo and Stitch become the best of friends. Lilo teaches Stitch to dance, play the guitar, and be more like Elvis. Most important, Lilo teaches him all about 'ohana—the Hawaiian word for "family"—meaning "no one gets left behind or forgotten."

step 1

STEP 2

STEP 3

PLEAKLEY

Agent Pleakley is your run-of-the mill nerdy alien. Because of his supposed knowledge of Earth, he is sent to capture Stitch. He tries to stick to the rules (which is hard with a partner like Jumba!). The always-uptight Pleakley spends much of his time panicking, worrying, and trying to prevent Jumba from destroying everything in sight.

STEP 1

Pleakley's 3 rounded legs are like tentacles, each with 2 fingerlike toes

legs are wider at waist and narrower at toes

STEP 2

FRONT VIEW

basic head shape fits into square

top section of head resembles a gum drop

SIDE VIEW   THREE-QUARTER VIEW

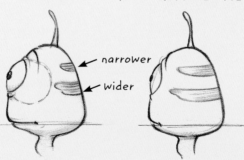

stripes on back of head lie behind single eye

narrower

wider

Pleakley is approximately 4 heads tall

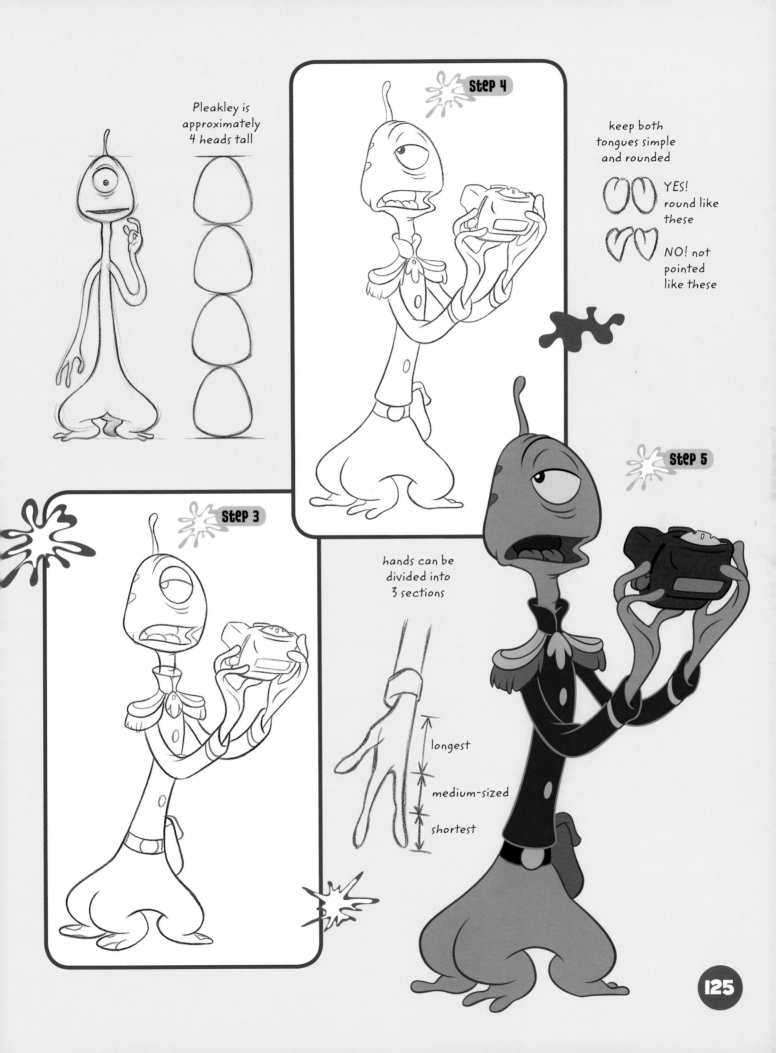

keep both tongues simple and rounded

YES! round like these

NO! not pointed like these

hands can be divided into 3 sections

longest

medium-sized

shortest

HOW·TO·DRAW

THE

LION KING

Illustrated by
David Pacheco
Diana Wakeman

The Making of *The Lion King*

In 1994, The Walt Disney Company released *The Lion King*, an enchanting movie about a young lion cub and his adventures on the African savannah. Many of Disney's previous movies were based on old, well-known stories. Here was a new story with all new characters. It would be up to the Disney animators to make Simba, Timon, Scar, and the rest of the animals as memorable as their predecessors.

The story of Simba revolves around the Circle of Life—the balance of nature and the bonds that tie all creatures together. In order to mirror the natural beauty of the animals and their habitats, Disney artists traveled to east Africa. In addition to sketching the animals and plants native to the region, they were able to observe the traditions and customs of the people who live there. Lions and other wild animals were also brought directly to the Disney studios to act as live models.

This intense research made it possible for *The Lion King* animators to capture the diverse sights, sounds, and moods of the African plains.

Photo by Gene Trindi

The Lion King was the first Disney film since *Bambi* to feature an all-animal cast. In some ways, the animal characters were easier to draw than humans. More liberties could be taken with their physiques and sizes, and there were no clothes to worry about!

Simba, the star of the movie, starts out as a bouncy, playful lion cub. His round belly, large paws, wide-set eyes and expressive tail convey his youth and energy. A tuft of fur on top of his head gives him a scruffy, childlike look.

ROUGH MODEL SHEET
YOUNG SIMBA
PRODUCTION 0885
"King of the Jungle" 1/13/92

129

Simba's cruel uncle Scar has a "lean and hungry" look. His claws are always visible and the scar over his left eye is a reminder of his violent streak. Animators experimented with placing the scar on different parts of his body before realizing that it couldn't be missed if placed directly on his face. Look carefully, and you will see similarities to Jafar from *Aladdin*.

A scar for Scar.

Timon the meerkat is the quintessential wise guy. Early drawings of him were very realistic, but then animators softened his appearance by changing his long claws to hands and making his tiny, pointy nose larger and rounder. His expressive eyebrows mimic those of Nathan Lane, the actor who gave him a voice.

An early drawing of Timon and the final version.

The African landscape was another important element in *The Lion King*. Whether they were painting brilliant sunsets or dark jungles, the artists sought to use background colors to convey emotion in a scene. Romance was a velvety blue, adventure was bold reds and golds, and humor was cheerful hues of green. The colors of the animals were also important. Most wild animals are shades of brown, so the artists tried to bring brighter colors to their palettes whenever they could. Rafiki started out with the facial features of a baboon, but in the final version, his colorful face is more like a mandrill's.

Audiences turned out in record numbers to see *The Lion King*, and they were not disappointed. The animation was unsurpassed, fulfilling the many hours of research and hard work involved.

A Disney artist draws from a model of Rafiki.

Photo by Mike Ansel

Simba's Head

Energetic young Simba just can't wait to be king. See if you can capture some of his enthusiasm in your drawing.

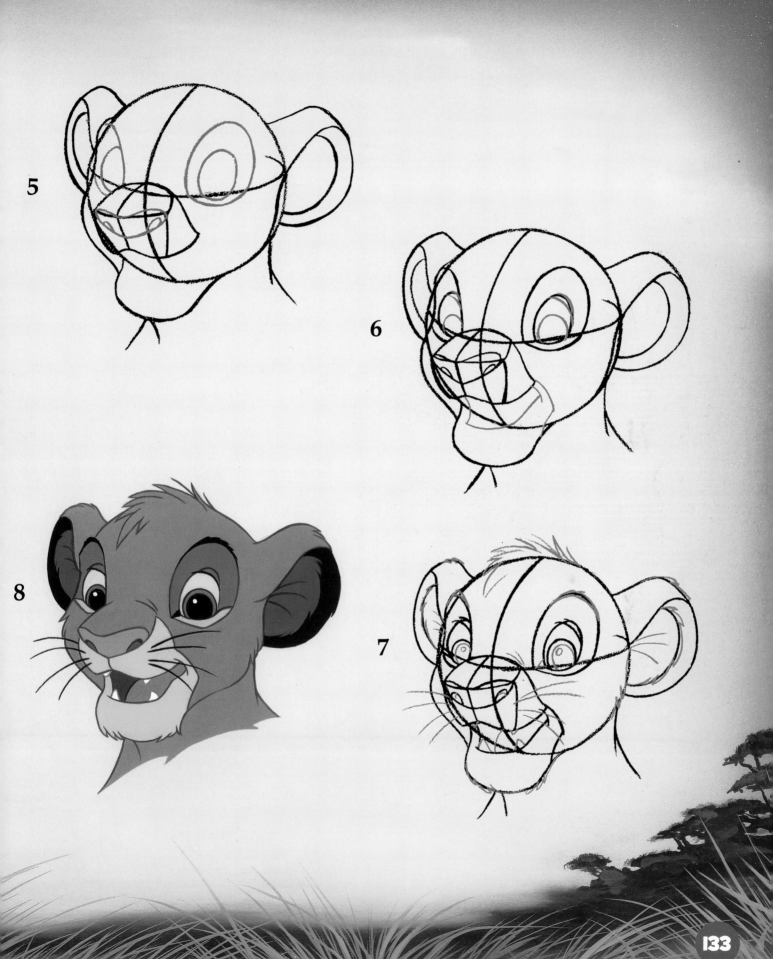

5

6

8

7

Young Simba, Full Body

Young Simba has a round, kittenish body, but he already shows signs of the king he is to become.

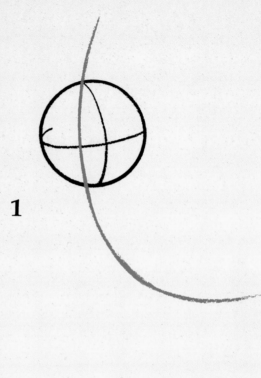

1

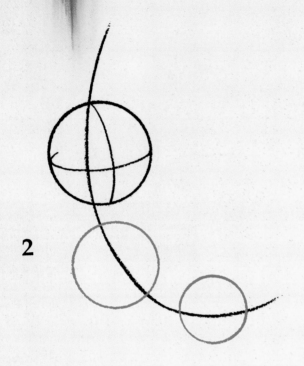

2

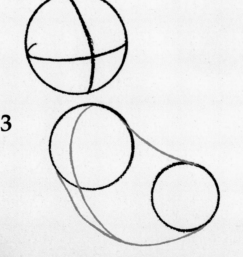

3

4

8

7

6

Scar's Head

The wicked Scar has a large nose and small eyes. His mane is darker and wilder than the other lions' manes, and his mouth curves in an evil grin.

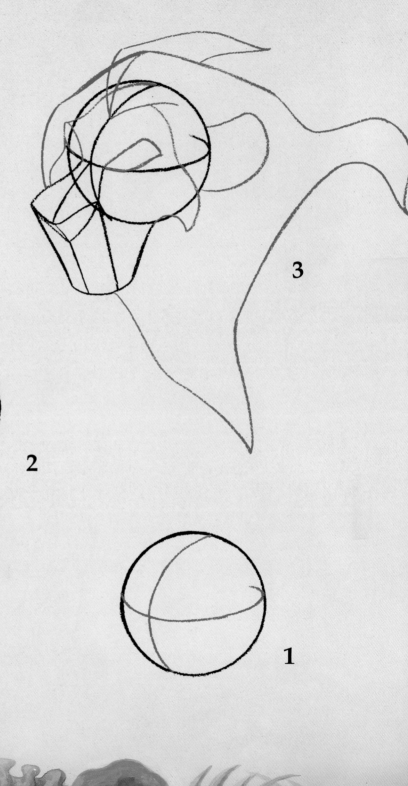

3

2

1

Remember that the scar runs across Scar's left eye.

4

5

6

Pumbaa, Full Body

It's no surprise that the biggest part of Pumbaa is his mouth!
This fun-loving warthog is one big smile.

1

2

3

4

5

6

7

8

Timon, Full Body

Timon's small body hides the biggest heart in the jungle.
He's little and quick, so draw him with short, quick lines.

4

5

6

Keep Timon's body lean, and his expressive face (eyes, mouth, and nose) BIG!

Adult Simba's Head

Simba grows up to become a brave, proud leader. Be sure to capture his regal bearing when drawing his head.

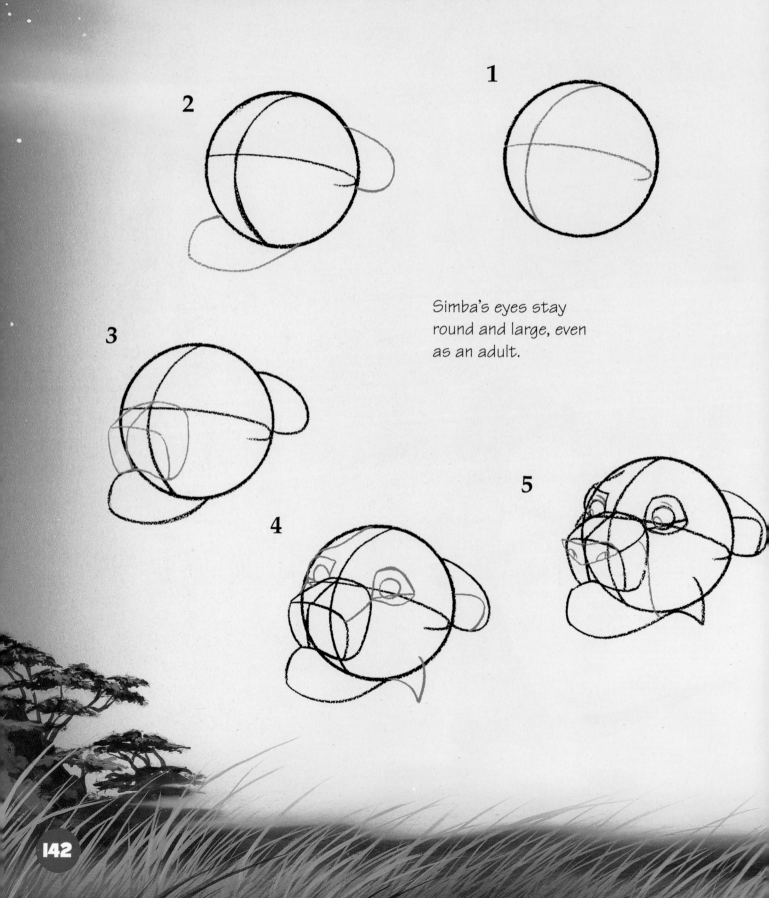

Simba's eyes stay round and large, even as an adult.

8

7

6

The End

www.walterfoster.com
Designed and published by Walter Foster Publishing, Inc.
3 Wrigley, Suite A, Irvine, CA 92618

Printed in China.